A YEAR
IN THE SUN

A YEAR IN THE SUN

MICHAEL VAUGHAN

with Martin Hardy

CORONET BOOKS

Hodder & Stoughton

The right of Michael Vaughan to be identified as the Author of the Work has been asserted by him in accordance with the Copyright, Designs and Patents Act 1988.

A Coronet paperback

1 3 5 7 9 10 8 6 4 2

A CIP catalogue record for this title is available from the British Library

ISBN 0 340 83095 6

Typeset in Linotype Sabon by
Rowland Phototypesetting Ltd,
Bury St Edmunds, Suffolk
Printed and bound by
Mackays of Chatham Ltd,
Chatham, Kent

Hodder Headline's policy is to use papers that are natural, renewable and recyclable products and made from wood grown in sustainable forests. The logging and manufacturing processes are expected to conform to the environmental regulations of the country of origin

Hodder and Stoughton Ltd
A division of Hodder Headline
338 Euston Road
London NW1 3BH

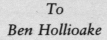

To
Ben Hollioake

CONTENTS

PHOTOGRAPHIC ACKNOWLEDGEMENTS

The author and publisher would like to thank the following for permission to reproduce photographs:

Philip Brown, Colorsport, Patrick Eagar, Getty Images/Allsport, Popperfoto.com/Reuters, Topham Picturepoint/Press Association.

ACKNOWLEDGEMENTS

This is the most difficult chapter in the book to write because so many different people have helped me throughout my life and career that I am bound to forget some of them. To those who have assisted and have been accidentally and unintentionally omitted, I offer my sincere apologies and thanks.

There are those who it is impossible to forget or thank enough and top of that list must come my parents, Graham and Dee, without whom none of this would have been possible. I could not have asked for a better or more supportive mother and father. They have encouraged rather than pushed, guided rather than led and supported rather than spoiled. No son could have asked for more and I will be eternally grateful. Hopefully some of the memorabilia they now possess from around the cricketing world will act as a constant reminder of my appreciation. My brother David has been just as much a friend to me and his help and backing cannot be overestimated.

There are other members of the family and a multitude of friends in Sheffield and elsewhere, too many to mention, who have helped in so many different ways and I would like them to know that their assistance and friendship is always appreciated.

Because this book is only about a small if eventful section of my life, I decided that it would be appropriate to dedicate it to the memory of my former England colleague Ben Hollioake, whose tragic death while the team were on tour in New Zealand during the early part of 2002 is still mourned by all who were close to him and remains a sad reminder that my year in the sun was not without its darker days.

I could easily have dedicated the book to Nichola, the girl who made me the proudest man on earth when she agreed to be my wife. She has always been there for me, even while pursuing her own career within the National Health Service, and given the number of injuries I have sustained to date, she could not have been involved with a more appropriate institution. I am sure she will forgive me, but the greatest dedication I can make to her is my entire life and that I will be doing shortly after this book goes on general release.

To the many doctors, nurses and physiotherapists who have pieced together and manipulated my body when it has been ravaged by injury and the world's fastest bowlers, I am sure they realise that every run I score is partially down to them. I am deeply indebted to their skills and professionalism.

I have a host of friends within the England, Yorkshire and some other county dressing rooms – and even the Australian ranks – whose camaraderie and fellowship I have thoroughly enjoyed, but I must single out one player for special mention. Martyn Moxon was my captain when I came into the Yorkshire dressing room and nobody could have made me more welcome or offered more advice and help than he did. Many of the cricketing values I will hold dear throughout my career are down to him for he is a perfect role model for every youngster entering the game.

I hope I have been able to thank my England colleagues at some stage during the book, but I must single out captain Nasser Hussain and coach Duncan Fletcher for all their support and guidance. My appointment as England's one-day captain will, I hope, reflect well on them. Nasser has always been extremely professional in the way he has tackled the job while I have not come across a better coach than Fletch particularly in the area of how to play spin.

Away from cricket, my business affairs are carefully looked after by Chubby Chandler and his team, including former England hero Neil Fairbrother, at International Sports Management. I am also indebted to Hodder and Stoughton for providing me with the platform to put my thoughts on an unbelievable year into book form, particularly their own Roddy Bloomfield, whose enthusiasm knows no bounds. He will undoubtedly dine out on how he clinched the deal for this book literally seconds before the surgeon about to perform a hip replacement operation on him confiscated his mobile phone.

Finally, my thanks to journalist and author Martin Hardy, who tore himself away from the Hop Blossom in Farnham and Sporting Index's spread betting pages to put my words and thoughts into order, in between mouthfuls of Madras curry at his beloved Boukara Indian Restaurant in Cape Town.

PREFACE

There had been little in my Test career prior to the start of the Sri Lanka series in 2002 to suggest that I would have a year in the sun quite like the one it turned out to be. Indeed, I returned from New Zealand before our summer programme realising that my apprenticeship in the international arena was now over and it was about time I started improving an average that was unlikely to keep me in the England side for much longer.

What followed was almost unbelievable. The sun and the runs arrived in a never-to-be-forgotten year. My confidence grew and twelve months later I had amassed a record number of runs, scored three Ashes centuries and been voted Man of the Series Down Under, become the first cricketer to appear on the front cover of Wisden, deposed Australia's Matthew Hayden as the world's number one batsman and been appointed England's one-day captain. And something I will treasure forever – I had possession of the ball with which I clean bowled the Master, Sachin Tendulkar, at Trent Bridge.

Going back over the year has refreshed many wonderful memories and I have thoroughly enjoyed being able to put down my thoughts and feelings about a time in my career that will live with me long into retirement. I hope there will be plenty more Test runs to come.

CHAPTER 1

HANDS OFF

Touring India was nothing new to me after first having visited as an eighteen-year-old playing for England Under 19s. Two years later, in 1995, I was there again with the A team, so in 2001 the views, exotic aromas, vivid colours, enchantment and passion of this cricket-mad nation were more than familiar. I am told that Spanish golfer Seve Ballesteros when once asked what it took to become a top player replied: 'The ability to eat at any table, sleep in any bed and perform on any course.' The same could easily be said about cricketers and especially those touring the subcontinent.

The learning curve of the teenage trip was an extensive one as we had four weeks on the road and three in the major cities. We did not stay at the best hotels in the world, we saw a lot of rats, there was very little air-conditioning and the food was, at best, average. I took as many tins of beans and Spam as I could and ate a lot of Snickers bars, but as an eighteen-year-old it was an experience that helped me mature more quickly as a cricketer than I might otherwise have done.

Indians do seem to establish themselves as players at a faster rate than we do and, like the Australians and South Africans, they are lobbed into the game during their teenage years to see if they can stand their ground against the best in the world. Perhaps the quick maturing of their cricketing skills has something to do with the way they are brought up on the subcontinent. I do know it is a fantastic place to tour because the love of cricket is unbelievable.

One thing I discovered early on, the curries bear very little resemblance to the ones served in Bradford. I will never forget staying at the beautiful Raj hotel in Bombay in 2001, straight opposite the Gates of India, and they did have a magnificent curry house. We sat on our knees on a cushion and ate the local way, although I wondered at first whether we were going to eat at all because when we sat down there was no cutlery. I had never eaten just with a chapatti before.

I have always thought it important to embrace the local culture wherever you travel because the last thing you want when you are away from home for any length of time is to stay in every night eating cheese and onion toasties. I had heard that it would be a boring tour with a lot of four-wall and television gazing, but that was not the case.

However, India is definitely the place to bring a touring party together. There are fewer distractions or attractions than in other places, and no bars outside the hotels, so a lot of time is spent in the team room taking the mickey out of one another. Unlike Australia, where everybody seems to have family or friends and there is always lots to do, India offers a greater bonding experience because you tend to stay as a unit more and create your own entertainment and banter, whether it is in the team room, dressing room or on the coach. No other tour generates that type of atmosphere.

So I knew exactly what to expect, although the 2001–02 tour was different in more than one respect. There was a stack of controversy before we left due to security concerns following the September 11 catastrophe in America. Television and the media kept everybody informed about what was happening in the subcontinent on a daily basis, while meetings went on for weeks leading up to the tour. Two of our players, Andrew Caddick and Robert Croft, decided, for family reasons, that the risks outweighed the advantages and stayed at home. They had the full backing of the players who did make the trip. Each individual has to make his own decision and these two concluded it was not in their interests to travel.

My decision to go was not taken lightly. Unless I have to make an instant assessment, I always like to hear the views of a number of people, not least my parents Graham and Dee, and my girlfriend Nichola. There were other considerations. A knee injury had kept me out of the Ashes series the previous summer and this was my opportunity to force my way back into the team. It would also be a great honour to play against the talents of Sachin Tendulkar, Sourav Ganguly and Rahul Dravid in their own backyard. I determined that whatever fate had in store for me, it could deal its hand in India and not at home in Sheffield.

With Caddick and Croft missing, two youngsters were handed the opportunity of some invaluable experience that would not otherwise have been available to them. Richard Dawson, my Yorkshire county colleague, took the spinner's position and performed admirably in all the Tests, while the vacant fast bowler's slot went to Richard Johnson, who did not get a great deal of opportunity to turn his arm over, but still picked up a helpful insight into the international game.

My experience of India convinced me that the public there would open their arms and hearts to an England touring side, especially after there had been doubt about whether or not one would arrive. The public's support was unbelievable. Any excursion out of the team hotel would prompt a friendly and enthusiastic crowd to gather around, while we knew every stadium would be jam-packed. It is just a fantastic country to play cricket in.

Having missed out against Australia, I was chomping at the bit to play international cricket again, but the first Test did not provide the opportunity. I was not selected, which left me wondering when and where the opportunity would arrive to strap on my pads and improve on a less-than-desired average of about 30.

The answer came at 11 p.m. on the eve of the second Test in Ahmedabad. There was a knock on the door of my room and I opened it to find Nasser Hussain standing outside, waiting to tell me that I was back in the team. Graham Thorpe had decided to return home because of things that were happening in his personal life.

Graham's misfortune was my good luck. I knew Graham was having problems. I'm pretty close to the Surrey left-hander and the two of us, along with another good friend, Ashley Giles, played a lot of PlayStation in India. We had our own football league – I was Manchester United, Graham was Chelsea and Ash was Arsenal. We had been playing that night and

I felt from the way he was acting that he was struggling with his situation. I thought he might take the option of going home to try to sort it out and so it was not really a surprise when Nasser came knocking on my door.

'You're playing and coming in at four,' he said.

I have played every Test since then, up to the time of writing.

I am a great believer in fate and also that things happen for a reason – one day you will be caught one-handed by somebody flying through the air on the boundary edge and the next you will dolly one straight to slip and see it put down. At the same time I can't help agreeing with golfer Gary Player when he said that the harder you practise, the luckier you get.

I was aiming to get a lot of runs on my Test comeback and I was not disappointed. Unfortunately, at the start, many of them were of the wrong variety. During the match in Ahmedabad I was forced to take up a position in the smallest room in the pavilion for long periods of the game. I do not think I have ever felt so ill in all my life.

There had been little warning of the discomfort ahead during our first innings when I was given out off Anil Kumble for 11 without ever getting near the ball. There was particular joy for Craig White as he hit a big hundred, for I knew very well how badly he wanted that innings. I remembered him getting 90-odd in Pakistan in 2000 and coming out saying: 'That might be the last chance I get to hit a century.' I had reassured him by saying: 'No, no, you'll get another chance.' And now he had proved me right. We all learned from the way he played that fantastic Ahmedabad innings and it helped set us up for the rest of the series against India. White had spotted something in Kumble's action during certain balls and he told us all about it and that was a tremendous benefit.

As for me, I spent all the second day in the dressing room with a towel over my head and needing to go to the bathroom every half hour. I was desperate to get out into the field and during one drinks break when the players were in a huddle, I walked out to join them. Halfway there Nasser saw me and yelled out: 'Get back, you're not coming out here like that,' so I turned round and went to bed again.

The suffering eased sufficiently the following day to allow me to bat and I remember getting 31 not out on a wicket where the ball was turning square. That positive knock gave me the confidence to go out and play that way on a more regular basis.

By the time we reached Bangalore for the third Test I was fit and ready for anything. We were 1–0 down in the series, but the nets went well and I sensed that things were about to change. The pitch was a little green, but it was a good one and I was playing for England as well as I had ever done.

I reached 64 with ease and was striking the ball beautifully, finding the gaps and dealing comfortably with the spinners. But just as I thought I was on the verge of a really big innings, my mind was sent into a spin when given out in the most bizarre of circumstances. I went to sweep Sarandeep, but the ball clipped my pads and rolled towards short leg. I don't know why I then did what I did because the ball was going nowhere near the stumps; I just flicked at it and then picked it up. It was an act of stupidity, but even when they appealed I was bemused because I did not know why they were appealing. I just did not understand why I had been given out. I was in a state of shock as I walked off, but then realisation kicked in that I'd been daft enough to handle the ball.

I compounded my misdemeanour by being a little naïve in that night's press conference. I said I was disappointed in the Indians' action, since the ball was not rolling back on to the stumps, but of course they were totally within their rights to appeal. I should have just held up my hands and said: 'I got it all wrong, I'm an idiot.' At least I learnt from the situation and particularly the press conference. I should never have let my heart do my thinking and talking, but I was simply pissed off because I was playing so well and I had passed up the perfect opportunity to get my first Test hundred outside England.

We had been in a good position and looking strong and then my stupidity undid all the good. Mark Ramprakash went in the next over and Andrew 'Freddie' Flintoff did not stay long. We were in the doghouse again, but then Craig White had another fine knock.

Freddie and Ashley Giles bowled us into a good position, but at the end of the second day clouds were beginning to gather and I remember saying to Nasser: 'These clouds have come to this part of the world for a reason.'

He just looked at me and said: 'It never rains in Bangalore.'

I knew he was going to be proven wrong.

Sure enough, we never bowled a ball on the last day because it bucketed down non-stop. It was so very frustrating because I felt we would have won the match and that would have meant a drawn series, never a bad result in India.

CHAPTER 2

SONG FOR BEN

The Christmas presents were barely out of their wrapping paper and New Year hangovers scarcely medicated before we were packing our whites and blues again. This time it was for New Zealand and a familiar face was among the party, of which he was always the life and soul.

Darren Gough is not only the dressing-room joker, but also the butt of quite a few jokes and he had been missed on the trip to India. It had been decreed by the powers that be that anybody who did not go to the subcontinent would not be considered for the Kiwi Tests of the winter, but my Yorkshire colleague was called in for the one-day series and was a very welcome addition to the squad.

It was good to have Gough back, not least for the confidence and spirit he brings to the dressing room. He is a lively character, who keeps everybody bubbling. He also comes out with some of the most extraordinary comments you have ever heard. They might not necessarily be the brightest thoughts, but at least they keep everybody entertained. To have his ability as a cricketer was also a big help. It cannot be over-estimated just how good a bowler he has been and one hopes will continue to be as long as his knees and legs can take the strain. In cricket's abbreviated version, Gough can be counted on to get at the top-order batsmen and then come back later to cool any advance when the willow is being heaved in every direction.

I was still learning about one-day cricket because my previous excursions in this particular department of the game had been limited. The approach to the one-day and five-day games is very similar, although experience in the shorter discipline is a massive thing, particularly if you bat in the middle of the innings. Every situation is different from the one you have faced just before and the one you will next encounter. You have no idea if the side will be a hundred for none after twenty-five overs when you go in, or 2 for 2 in the first over.

A decent cricket brain is essential because you have to adapt to whatever the situation is and this was one of my initial shortcomings. Early in my career, my cricket thinking was not as clever as it should have been, but now I have my head round most situations and I know the value of building partnerships or re-grouping to get the team back on track. The middle of the innings may be the hardest time to bat, but it is also the most fascinating.

I have always been my own harshest critic, but the reason I am hard on myself is because I want to be the best. Whatever standard you are playing at, you can always be better. The day when I start being too easy on myself will be the one when it is time to stop because I will have reached the stage where I do not want to progress any further.

I am tough on myself, but I am that way because it pushes me towards constant improvement – something I chase not purely for personal enhancement, but because I want the team to win as many games as it can. To be successful either individually or collectively you have to be honest with yourself and I am always that because it helps me and the team improve.

Ranting and raving and shouting at people is not my style, but I cannot sit back and say 'It's just a game of cricket' if I play a bad shot or do something wrong. Whether I am playing or practising or even just thinking about the game, I do like to do things well.

If I have a bad day or hit a bad shot, I'll think about what has happened, analyse everything and then work on eradicating the flaw or problem. Once I wake up the following morning I am ready to move on to the next issue.

The best sportsmen in the world are pretty harsh on themselves, although they do not get too dejected when things are not working out or too involved or over-excited when they are. They get through the good or bad times by staying on an even keel, not allowing themselves to soar up in the clouds or be sucked deep down in the mud. Those who prosper stay on a level playing field all the time. That way you can cope with excitement and disappointment much better than if you are bouncing off the walls or ready to dial the Samaritans.

Ever since I was about eighteen, I have always looked, listened and learned from the way people act in certain situations. I watch when players are scoring runs to see how they act with others, how they talk to the media and how it changes them. On the reverse side, I look at the way people deal with failure to the extent that now I believe I can judge a player by the way he reacts when he is playing badly. I like those characters who still get involved, continue laughing and take the game exactly the same when the ball is not finding the middle of the bat or the proper line and length. They seem to have the best perspective on life as a cricketer.

When life gets tough the media and even friends jump on your back and you get the occasional comment in the street. The next time a Yorkshire voice tells me to 'Bugger off back to Lancashire' will not be the first. The strong characters are those who can laugh off the bad times, not only knowing they will come through them, but also realising there are good times around the corner.

I quickly discovered that Yorkshire is a fantastic place in which to be schooled as a cricketer. Discipline both on and off the field – lifestyle, fitness, punctuality and dress code – has always been a major issue. Looking smart and shaving every day have been driven into me since I was a kid and I must say it has stood me in good stead. The most disciplined teams on and off the pitch are always the most victorious. It is no surprise that Manchester United and Arsenal are as successful as they are.

Steve Oldham, a great disciplinarian, who never accepted an excuse for anybody being late, knocked the virtue of punctuality into me at Yorkshire. Lateness was unacceptable because it meant you were letting your team-mates down. It sounds a bit old-fashioned in today's world and I have sometimes wondered if it really does matter that much, but the more I play and the more I think about it, the players who are successful and the ones who stay at the top longest are the ones who are the most disciplined.

The number one example is Alec Stewart. At the time of

writing, he is thirty-nine, has played top-class cricket since he was eighteen and been in the England team for the last fourteen years, and he is the most disciplined man I have ever met, a great role model. If you want to get to the top in any sport, be it cricket, golf, rugby, football or tiddlywinks, then do no more than look at the way Stewart looks, acts and behaves. He is immaculate on and off the pitch. He possesses genuine star quality, and because of it gets plenty of stick from his colleagues – as well as the utmost respect.

I remember first coming into the Yorkshire dressing room and Martyn Moxon was exactly the same. He was so disciplined he would set out his kit and would know if anybody had moved one of his things just half an inch. Unfortunately, I am not like that. I have a big Nike bag and everything just gets lobbed out in a pile.

Stewart just could not be like that. He has his shoes on a ledge; caps, gloves, sweaters and bats are all in place. He is nearly teetotal, has a great diet and is one of our fittest players. We call him the Governor because he governs everything and it seems that whatever he wants he gets – quite rightly so when you consider what he has done and the number of matches he has played. He knows how to go about it. At the 2003 World Cup's opening ceremony in Cape Town he was quite hungry and asked if I fancied some food. 'Follow me,' he said and within minutes he had found a chef who served up chicken and mash for us just as quickly.

I dread to think what it is going to be like when he goes because he is going to be one hell of a cog in our machine to replace. He drills discipline into the team, although he is not a guy who says you must do this or follow that ideal – he just gets on with his own job and leads by example. Men of that calibre are a rarity and one thing is definite, there will never be another like him.

After India and its very limited nightlife, we arrived in New Zealand for three Tests and five one-day internationals and we were faced with a week between games. Time for a bit of r & r. It is essential, not least for your sanity, to let your hair down now and again, but nobody had told Paul Collingwood that to enter on such an excursion with Freddie Flintoff could seriously damage your health, particularly in the region of the liver. Freddie is world ranked number one when it comes to letting your hair down.

I saw the two of them leaving the team hotel and just thought to myself, are you sure you know what you are doing, Paul? I turned up an hour later, looked at Collingwood's eyes and knew instantly that he had been what is commonly called Flintoffed. Collingwood discovered the hard way how trying to keep pace with Freddie can result in a monumental hangover.

My services were not required for the first three one-day games, but I netted very well indeed and was called up for the fourth in Auckland. Going in at five I scored a quick 64, but, not for the first time that winter, I was out in controversial circumstances.

Going for a quick run, I managed to drop my bat and the decision on whether I had made my ground was referred to the third umpire. As we awaited the verdict, the umpire indicated to me that he had heard from the third official that I was out, so I just walked off. I was actually getting vibes that I was not out and when I got into the dressing room my suspicions were confirmed. I was officially 'not out', but I had walked off and it was a bit too late to do anything about it. The words 'complete' and 'idiot' spring to mind. It was so frustrating because I had been desperate to get my place back for three weeks and, having been recalled to the side, I had been playing beautifully, hitting the ball to all parts. Now I looked nothing less than stupid at a time when I was trying to establish myself in both forms of the game.

It gets asked of any new player in a team, is he a Test player, a one-dayer or can he play both? There were those who thought at the time that maybe I was just a five-day specialist and perhaps they had a point. In those more tentative days, I was more concerned about occupying the crease than scoring runs. Mentally, I believed that if I stayed out there, the runs would come eventually. What a difference a year makes! Now I have a completely different mindset. When I am at the crease I am thinking, positively, that I will score runs rather than waiting for them to come to me. Before, I had been trying to accumulate them and my first 50 would take two to three hours. Now I try to hit every bad ball, wanting to score every time, and the runs come faster. Because I was an accumulator, people said I was not suited to the one-day game, but I always knew I had the shots that would serve me well. I just had to be more confident and positive about my ability to play shots, and try to dictate to the bowlers rather than worry too much about survival.

It can be hard to adapt at first, especially with the pressure imposed by, the media and expectation levels. You must have that inner belief that you can adapt. The first few games are extremely difficult because you are feeling your way and there are so many ups and downs. The mental game is important, building yourself up and getting yourself right for the event.

At least I had 64 on the board before my mental aberration and then we went out to field. I had been dropping catches of late – indeed my catching had been embarrassingly bad for a couple of years – but my confidence rose when I caught two early in their innings. Then, in the fiftieth over, I went for a diving catch on the boundary and my shoulder popped out. It was the worst feeling I had ever had. It clicked straight back in, but there was damage, which kept me out of the final and deciding game, and it seemed that I might miss the first Test.

Our physiotherapist and medical staff did much manipulation and work, but the shoulder was very tender for three weeks. If there was frustration for me, there was agony for Darren Gough in the deciding game, which we lost. He came off the pitch and said: 'My knee's gone, that's it.' He has played very little since. Gough was going home injured and it dented the spirit of the tour. His absence has always left the England dressing room with a big void.

The tour was damaged, but not irreparably. Michael Atherton, Nasser Hussain and Alec Stewart had always told me that the New Zealand trip was the best of the lot because of the climate, similar to England's, hospitable people, great golf and wine and usually competitive cricket. You could let your hair down a bit more there and the golf was certainly good for practising wind shots.

If the golf was excellent, the wine Andy Caddick recommended was of similar calibre. He is a connoisseur, or thinks he is, and the vintages he chose were always spot on, particularly those that he served when the entire party went for a barbecue to the house he has in what is, after all, his homeland.

The girlfriends and wives were with us for a lot of the trip, although the weather was such that they did not do a great deal more than shop. One of the highlights for me was meeting Britain's Admiral's Cup yacht team. We watched them train and went on the boat. Flintoff and Caddick actually went out with them to get a taste of life on the ocean waves. It was very interesting to watch professionals from another sport and I had no idea just how much money and effort are put into the project. They earned everybody's respect.

The New Zealand Test team earned everybody's approbation, as well. Under Stephen Fleming the Kiwis are a good, decent and competitive side who play the game as it should be played and respect opponents.

The first National Bank Test in Christchurch was a landmark in my career because I opened for England for the first time at this level – resurrecting the partnership I had had at Under 19 level with Marcus Trescothick. I had played with Trescothick for years and our understanding was there straightaway.

I remember having one reservation when Nasser said I would open in Christchurch. It was nothing to do with my opening partner, but the pitch we would bat on – one of those drop-in wickets they put in place four or five days in advance. When we went to the ground to practise a couple of days before the game, I remember thinking that it was strange that the wicket had not arrived – but it had. Close inspection showed that it was a strip of mud, and soft to boot. I just knew it would not have dried out before the game and here I was preparing to open for the first time. This would be tough, particularly for the side batting first.

Everybody knew the toss was crucial because the wicket was still damp and the silver lining in the clouds overhead was for the side bowling first. Win the toss and bowl ... and that is exactly what New Zealand did. Walking out to bat was a quiet journey. Trescothick and I decided we would run as hard as we could between the wickets to try to put them under pressure.

They were the last few words we said to one another during that partnership because within two balls of Chris Cairns' first over Trescothick was walking back to the pavilion, followed by Mark Butcher a couple of balls later. This was my first Test as an opener and I had already had two partners without having had the chance to say a word to either of them at the end of an over.

My first chat with a partner was with the captain. I asked him what he thought and he was very reassuring. 'We're in the shit,' he said. Nasser does not mince words. I hit my second ball for six, hit a four and then reached 27 off twenty-odd balls before nicking one off Cairns. As I walked off, I was convinced we would be rolled over on that track for less than a hundred. If they bowled even half well we just did not have a chance. Thankfully, Nasser proved me wrong and batted unbelievably well.

When it's backs-to-the-wall stuff, the ball's seaming and the opposition are completely on top, Nasser will always come to the fore. People talk about my hundreds and, all right, they were good, but they were made on good wickets. Nasser Hussein's hundred on a wicket that was damp and zipping was nothing short of incredible, especially after coming in second wicket down without a run on the board. Just how much hard labour he had to put into that marathon can be seen from the statistics. His 50 came from 113 balls – nineteen of those when he was on 49 – and his tenth Test century took 307 minutes. The only 'life' he had was when Stephen Fleming spilled one at first slip when he was 52.

Nasser, last man out on 106, drew inspiration from watching Australia's Ricky Ponting on television that morning scoring a ton. Apparently, he said to himself it was about time he did the same after a succession of scores between 30 and 80. Never has the term captain's innings been more appropriate.

Our innings was not helped by a couple of umpiring decisions that were at best debatable. Mark Ramprakash was given out caught behind off a ball that missed his bat by the width of it and in fact clipped the top of his pad. Andy Caddick was another victim when he was adjudged lbw off Ian Butler when an inswinging yorker looked as if it was heading towards fine leg.

How we got to 228 on that terror track I will never know, but that innings set us up for the game. Matthew Hoggard pepped up our spirits when he removed dangerous Kiwi opener Mark Richardson to leave our hosts on 9 for 1 in reply at the end of the first day.

Hoggard, backed by a fine spell from Caddick, continued his good work on the resumption and finished with 7 for 63, making the most of his ability to swing the ball. With Caddick taking the other three in the space of five balls, it meant that

New Zealand were all out for 147 leaving us 81 runs ahead and feeling we were in control of our own destiny. We took an advantage of 144 into the third day with 8 wickets to fall.

After my first-innings knock, I was pretty confident when I went out to bat for the second time. Three balls later Ian Butler went through my defences for what was the eighth duck of the match and I was on my way back to the pavilion, ruefully thinking that, after being given the opening I had wanted for what seemed like such a long time, I'd let people down. My job had been to set up the middle order and I had not delivered. What we did with the new ball was crucial and I had been out to an average shot.

Help for the team was at hand. Graham Thorpe, dropped from the second ball he faced, made New Zealand pay for the mistake by scoring the third fastest Test double hundred (off 231 balls) and then Freddie Flintoff had something to celebrate after walking out on a pair and totally lacking any confidence. 'It just can't get any worse,' he said to me before going out to bat, but he murdered them, just as Mark Butcher did against Australia in the fifth Test when he was in the middle of a deep slump. I looked at those knocks and thought that it does not matter what has gone before; every time you walk to the wicket there is a chance of a ton.

It was great to have Thorpe back on board. He had sorted out a few problems off the field and decided it was time to play cricket again. To score a double hundred after the predicament he had found himself in over the previous three months was unbelievable. It was typical of him that he should dedicate a ton each to his two children. All the team were delighted for him and I think he realised just how much everybody was behind him from our response when he reached three figures. It was a full-attendance standing ovation from the players' balcony.

Freddie's ton at the Jade Stadium, Christchurch, was his maiden Test century and came from just 114 balls, and his partnership with Thorpe added 281 for the sixth wicket – a record for any team against the Kiwis. The wicket had improved out of all recognition and we knew when New Zealand went looking for the 550 we set them to win, that they might be capable of getting somewhere near.

It looked like we would coast to an easy victory when we reduced them to something like 180 for 6, but Nathan Astle decided to have a little bit of fun at Caddick's, who bowled exceptionally well in the circumstances, and Hoggard's expense. They did not see the funny side of his onslaught. He started despatching them, and anybody else who got hold of the ball, out of the ground. From being masters of our own destiny, all of a sudden we were staring at humiliation. I would love to have had a picture of our field at one point during the carnage because, apart from bowler, stumper and slip, everybody else was on the boundary edge and we still could not stop Astle finding the gaps. This match has gone, I said to myself at one point. Fortunately, we were spared and finally forced a win by 98 runs, but not before Astle had broken the world record for the fastest double hundred by an incredible fifty-nine balls – and he had hit only seventy-four scoring shots in his 222.

Full marks to Thorpe, Hoggard and Flintoff, but the real

hero was Nasser Hussain – to have hit a hundred in the first innings on that track was nothing short of awesome.

Nasser and I have our differences, but I respect him as a captain and understand what he has to put up with. I also have the highest regard for him as a batsman because he is definitely a player you want in your team when the going gets tough. As for some of his antics on the pitch – shaking his head and kicking the dirt when somebody drops a clanger – well, I do not think I would do that, but that is the way he does his job and I have always felt that captain and coach should be allowed to do what they have to do in the way they want to do it.

You have to acknowledge that Nasser might kick the dirt or shake his head from time to time. You have to be strong enough as a player to look him in the eye and say: 'Sorry, I did my best, but I let you down a bit there.' I do not think he minds, as long as you do try as hard as you can, but he does get mad when he feels players are not doing themselves or the team justice. He starts his head shaking when he feels players are losing concentration and not doing their job.

In Australia he got a lot of stick about it because Down Under they say you must always back your team-mates, whatever they are doing. But that is the way Nasser is and we have come to accept it as a team. The first few games when he had a fit of histrionics, I found somewhat nerve-racking, but I have come to accept that he wants what is best for English cricket.

As for drop-in wickets, our game in England may even benefit from them, although I do believe that to transplant one just four days before the match, as happened in Christchurch, was a little too close to the first over. With drop-in wickets there would be so many more uses the ground could be put to; the amount of time and money we spend putting up stadia compared with the amount of use they get does not make sense.

But the made-to-measure pitches do have to be of a high standard because Test match cricket is about endurance, concentration and trying to outmanoeuvre your opponents on a good wicket. It is no good if the wicket does it for you and that was the case initially in the first Test.

I should know a thing or two about interesting tracks because of my experience at Headingley where there is never a dull moment at Test time. Although the bounce is uneven I do think it is a magnificent Test match wicket because you do have to work on your technique to bat on it.

The first few years I played there, I reckon I made the excuse of the wicket as a reason why I did not score many runs. I blamed the pitch and I was convinced the only way to improve was to leave Yorkshire. I came very close a few times because I felt I would never improve if the track did not.

I was in my early twenties, trying to break into the England set-up. I was going on the A tours, then coming back and never scoring the runs like the guys down south or at Old Trafford. I blamed the wicket when I now believe the only thing at fault was my attitude. All in all, not getting into the England team until 1999 when I was twenty-three probably did me good. By then I was ready; any earlier might have been too soon.

Things do happen for a reason, I believe, and maybe not scoring runs at Headingley was telling me that I was not ready for the big stage, that my technique was still not good enough for cricket at the highest level. They say golfers blame their caddies and their clubs when things go wrong; cricketers blame the bats, wicket, weather and umpires. You name it and we will hold it responsible for our misfortunes instead of saying: 'I'm not playing well here, I'm not doing the right things, my technique's not great and my attitude stinks.' That is why I was averaging only 30 in county cricket at the time.

I had only myself to blame for my second-innings duck in that first Test at Christchurch, but at least we won the match and rule number one when that happens is that the success has to be celebrated – not that many of us felt like too many glasses. The atmosphere in the dressing room was decidedly downbeat after coming reasonably close to losing the match when we had been in complete control. It had been so mentally tiring chasing Astle's shots everywhere. But Freddie Flintoff relaxed the atmosphere by reminding us that we had actually won and soon we were all tranquil, some more spectacularly than others.

Moving on to Wellington for the second Test, my success as a Test opener continued to require a magnifying glass for inspection, especially among those who thought I had no right to be there in the first place. There were some who were still in mourning for Michael Atherton and my first three returns – 27, 0 and 7 – did little to ease their suffering. I was not particularly concerned about what others thought, but I must admit a few doubts started entering my head about whether I was up to the job, although the wickets we were playing on were making it hard for top-order batsmen with the ball seaming and swinging around.

I had always opened for Yorkshire, but it is such a huge gap between county and country and now I was starting to wonder if I could adapt. I refused to get too down on myself because not too many of our top order were getting runs.

My form problems were minuscule compared to the thunderbolt that was to rip through the England dressing room during the first session of the third day in Wellington. A text message came through to my mobile phone and I looked at it wondering what on earth it meant and hoping beyond hope that it was not anything nearly as serious as it seemed.

The message read: 'Sorry to hear about Ben Hollioake.' We had not heard a thing about Ben since he left after the one-day series – matches in which he had shown that his game was back on track and that he was likely to be a force in the World Cup.

I was sitting next to Ashley Giles, so I showed him the message and asked what he thought it meant. As I was speaking, Duncan Fletcher, who had heard us talking about it, came over and whispered in my ear that Ben had been killed in a car crash but could I keep it quiet until lunchtime because it was going to affect the morale of the people waiting to bat.

My own feelings were indescribable. I had known Ben and played with him for a long time, but obviously I was not as close as the Surrey boys in the party. Mark Butcher got out and the first he heard was from the television screen. You can imagine the shock that was relayed from the dressing room to the viewing area. We had to play the rest of the game when not one of us wanted to play at all. The spirit was never the same for the rest of the tour.

Tragedies like that do put cricket into perspective and, although I would not say that Ben's death changed my life and approach to cricket completely, it did have a profound effect.

It made me value family and friendships even more, especially among those who had always been there for me. It also made me see cricket for what it is, a game to be enjoyed while you are playing it. I am sure after Ben's death a lot of people realised the value of their own lives and it made them understand that you never know what fate has in store. It made me want to go out into the middle and enjoy the experience; collectively, it united us because we were definitely more relaxed about cricket.

We should have won that second Test, but nobody cared when we did not. The match was memorable for Ben's loss and nothing else, and nobody felt it more than his Surrey colleagues, Mark Butcher and Graham Thorpe. There were a lot of tears and emotion around the camp for the entire trip and the lads did well to get themselves up for any game.

Consideration was given to all of us going to Australia for the funeral, but because of the schedule it was deemed impractical, so Nasser went to represent us all. We were there in spirit and we staged our own memorial service on top of a hill outside Auckland. It was a quiet, secluded spot and Mark Butcher brought out his guitar and sang Bob Marley's 'Redemption Song' and said a few words, as did Phil Neale, the team's operations manager.

I think my approach to batting, while not moving from careful to carefree, did change. I did not become a totally free spirit and just go out to have a swing. That has never been and never will be my attitude, but I did decide that I needed to be more relaxed about it, whether I got nought going in on a pair or was able to carry on to a big score. The enjoyment factor allows you to play more shots as long as your technique is sound and you are in the right position to play them.

On the field of play the Wellington Test was memorable for little more than the amount of rain that fell and the speed of the wind that prevented any action on the first day – the umpires deciding at 12.30 that not a ball would be bowled. Indeed, it was not until 3.30 the following afternoon that I went out to bat and not for very long at that, Fleming taking me at slip off a Chris Drum delivery that seamed. Trescothick made an entertaining 37, while Butcher benefited more than most from the day and a half's delay because it allowed extra recovery time for the cracked thumb he received in the first Test. But nobody was really interested in cricket at a time when we had been reminded that there are far more important things in life.

To get to 220 for 4 was a reasonable achievement, but to lose the last 6 wickets for 60 more was not. Our fortunes increased considerably after that and we entered the final day with a 246-run lead and 105 overs to play with, thanks mainly to Trescothick and Butcher and a fast and furious knock by Flintoff, their efforts enabling us to give New Zealand 86 overs and a target of 356 – a task that proved beyond them as play ended with them on 158 for 4.

For the last Test in Auckland's Eden Park there was another portable wicket, and with a lot of rain around, the team bowling first, in this case us, was favoured. The weather, so reminiscent of home, allowed just 54 overs to be bowled on the first day and we restricted them to 151 for 5.

We had them struggling at 19 for 4 with Caddick becoming

the ninth English bowler to pass 200 wickets, but when Chris Harris was given not out on a bat-pad appeal it allowed them to recover and pass 200. We lost 2 early in reply and then I remember playing well again the following morning before snicking one behind, having made 27. It was the third time in the series that I had got out when I was set, and I was disappointed not to go on because my rhythm was as good as it had been all tour. We scraped to get just under their score on an iffy wicket.

As rain interfered for much of the next two days it looked like we would claim the series, but New Zealand are nothing if not fighters under Fleming, jokingly taunted by the Barmy Army as the worst captain in the world, and they ended the fourth day on 269 for 9, representing a 311-run advantage, a formidable target for us on a track with gremlins in it.

As I walked out with Trescothick, I remember saying: 'We'll have to get on top of them,' and I reached 36 very quickly. I felt this was the time for me to go on, make a score, win the match and show that I was a natural-born opener because of the approach I was taking. I was playing my shots, but unfortunately was undone by one. This was four times I had looked like making an 80 or a ton, but failed to do so. It was disheartening to have played a series without making a major contribution.

The Kiwis had not beaten us in a home series since 1984, but the last day would be theirs after setting us a target of 312 in 105 overs. After being 154 for 5, we fell 78 runs short and the series was drawn 1–1, although I felt we had played the livelier cricket and deserved better. It was an exciting match, but not what I call a proper one because of the conditions and pitch. Bowlers did not have to bowl well to take wickets, just put it somewhere near and let the pitch do the rest. To me, that is not Test match cricket.

Although there was a dark cloud of sadness because of the tragedy of Ben's death, there were pluses. James Foster, playing in only his second series, looked the part. Hoggard was the real star and Flintoff received rave reviews and looked as if he was going to push on and become the star we all know he can be. Trescothick and I were developing as a partnership, Butcher and Nasser Hussain were playing well and we were all kicking on and learning more about each other. So it was a valuable tour in some respects.

I was ready for home and felt jaded when I got there. I had no intention of looking at a bat for a while never mind picking one up, so I watched Sheffield Wednesday and Manchester United, played golf and moved house, a particular pain in the backside as anybody who has done it will know.

It was a time to chill out and then look forward to facing the Sri Lankans and the start of what was to become my summer-and-winter-long runfest.

CHAPTER 3
BEGINNING TO CLICK

The build-up to the first Test against Sri Lanka at Lord's did little to inspire me, or anybody else for that matter. I had not scored many runs for Yorkshire, nothing more than a 30 and I felt terrible. My game and head were just not there in any way and my technique bordered on terrible.

Marcus Trescothick wondered if I was trying to play too many shots, but I dismissed that suggestion. I believed it was just that my method was not getting me into position to either attack or defend and I felt I had two left feet. Something was definitely missing.

Still, I was not too despondent as I made my way to headquarters because my memories of Lord's were all good ones. I had scored a century against Middlesex and a commendable 40-odd against the West Indies when Mike Atherton and I put on 90-plus against Curtly Ambrose and Courtney Walsh on a juicy wicket.

But this was the start of another domestic international season and I would not be able to get by on memories alone, so when we all decanted from our trains, planes and cars and turned up for practice on Monday, I went up to Duncan

Fletcher, told him of my problems and concerns and asked him to have a good look at me in the nets. I knew we would be facing a lot of left-armers over the wicket and I needed my rhythm to be in perfect synchronisation.

Within four balls, Fletcher spotted a flaw, changed one little thing and everything just slotted into place. That is the kind of coach we have. He is a very shrewd watcher, keeps everything simple and knows most of the guys' games inside out. He noticed I was standing too open, my shoulders and body were facing towards mid-wicket instead of between mid-on and the bowler. The subtle change paid instant dividends. From that moment I started hitting the ball properly again and into the right areas. Defence and attack all clicked.

I spent two hours on the bowling machine with our physiologist Nigel Stockhill feeding me inswingers and I just grooved and grooved things until I felt I was ready to take on the world again.

No matter how well you play in practice and think you have it sussed out, when the game situation arrives it is a totally different environment. In the nets you feel caged, almost claustrophobic, but in the middle there are fielders – and gaps.

Even though I was happier with my technique, I was still more nervous than usual going into the match because I knew my figures in New Zealand were not up to scratch. The media were writing such things as: 'Right, this is the time. Michael Vaughan's had long enough in the international game, but he has to put together a string of scores as an opener should. He must move to the next level.' The point they were making in not too subtle tones was fair enough. I think a new player should have up to twelve Test matches and maybe more to feel his way in different environments and conditions, to get used to the whole international cricket scene and the greater intensity of everything. I had had sixteen matches and the jury was still out.

I knew I had to kick on because a massive hole had been left in the team with Atherton gone – not just because of his batting, but also his personality. I admire Mike massively, not simply for the way he batted, but also for the way he comported himself on the pitch. I know he got a bit of stick for the way he dealt with the media throughout his captaincy, and it is something of an irony that he works in that area now, but I always thought he was made of the right stuff both on and off the field.

In one way it was encouraging that people thought I could fill that gap, but I knew I could not play the way he did. Our techniques differed and I had also vowed to myself in New Zealand, even though the runs did not come as plentifully as I would have liked, that my approach would be the same throughout the summer. I was going to discover just where I could get with the power of positive thought and strokeplay. Nobody could become Michael Atherton, Michael Vaughan, Marcus Trescothick or anybody else. You have to be yourself . . . and I was going to be the new me.

I knew I was under pressure to score and it quickly became evident that we would have plenty of runs to chase after Sri Lanka skipper Sanath Jayasuriya won the toss and opted for first use of a pitch that may have been unpredictable at such an early stage of the season. It turned out to be a belter and the visitors wasted no time exploiting it.

Nobody enjoyed the conditions, pitch and day more than Marvan Atapattu and Mahela Jayawardene, batsmen out of the top drawer. It is not often that my fielding earns generous applause, but it received a good hand when Jayasuriya chanced his luck and my throw beat him home by a couple of inches. When Matthew Hoggard got one to lift against Sangakkara and Freddie Flintoff took the edge at second slip, we were confident that we could restrict our guests to a reasonable figure, but it would prove our last success until deep into the final session.

Atapattu, watchful but never slow to pounce on the loose ball, and Jayawardene tickled, pushed, drove and clubbed their way to excellent centuries, although I was sure I had secured another run out in the first over after lunch. Atapattu wanted a quick single as his partner pushed Hoggard wide of me at gully, but I threw the wicket down and was disappointed when, after lengthy deliberation, the third umpire, Jeremy Lloyds, ruled in the batsman's favour.

Apart from Jayawardene falling with about an hour to go, we had no further success. I left the field looking forward to my turn to play on a wonderful wicket. Its character did not change overnight and Atapattu went on to score 185. Backed by a big half century from Aravinda de Silva and a 50 from Russel Arnold, Sri Lanka amassed their biggest ever total at Lord's – Jayasuriya finally ending his side's innings on 555 for 8. It left us a tricky few overs to negotiate against Chaminda Vaas and Nuwan Zoysa, always dangerous with the new ball, and Trescothick was unable to survive, undone by a ball that left him down the slope, the Sri Lankan captain taking the catch off Zoysa at slip.

It could have been a confidence thing, but even though I had made that little change in my stance, my feet and timing were still not quite as I wanted them. That all changed with one ball when I was on 15. I played a cover drive against Vaas and it flew to the boundary. Ah, that's what it feels like, I said to myself. I had forgotten. It takes just one shot or movement to get your form and rhythm back and that was it. I remember leaning into the stroke and punching the ball through extra cover. I had not done it for a while and it certainly felt good. A while in cricket can be two weeks plus and if you go that long without finding your tempo it becomes a worry.

There was more where that shot came from and I played well in partnership with Nasser and then, as Graham Thorpe and I pushed the score beyond 200, it looked as if we could make hay while the sun did not shine on this particularly over-cast day. I was on 64 and went for a hook off Ruchira Perera, but got slightly under it and Zoysa did the rest at deep square leg. I took some stick for playing an attacking shot because there are still people who feel you should not get out that way. Not me. I would much prefer to get out while trying to score rather than when just trying to block my wicket.

After the game Perera was reprimanded for having a suspect action. I cannot really comment on whether he does throw the ball or not, but he definitely bowled with some decent pace that day, and troubled our batsmen. The ball he got me with came on to me a bit faster than I thought it would.

I really should have got a big score, but with my dismissal came a flood of them – Thorpe the next ball – and suddenly we were 203 for 5 and all out for not a great deal more, being forced to follow on some 280 in arrears. That first innings, however, really helped because I found my rhythm, feet and head. Now I was ready to play the kind of knock I knew I was capable of and everybody else was waiting for. I vowed to play better second time around.

When a side follows on, the opening stand assumes massive proportions. Lose an early wicket and the opposition get a lift and a Mexican wave of shudders floods through your own dressing room. Trescothick and I carried that awesome responsibility with us to the crease for the second time and we were fortunate enough to get the big numbers the team desperately needed.

Every batsman is vulnerable early in his innings and I am no exception. It was with immense relief that, after hitting Buddika for a couple of boundaries, I nicked one low to first slip and Jayasuriya spilled it, the same player committing the same offence off Zoysa when I was 33. The reprieves toughened my resolve as we dug in to put on a record opening wicket stand against Sri Lanka before Trescothick was given out in controversial fashion.

Replays clearly showed he had got an inside edge on to his pads, but the shouts for lbw were upheld by umpire Daryl Harper and we lost our first wicket on 168, the highest opening stand for four years since Michael Atherton and Mark Butcher scored 179 between them against South Africa at Edgbaston. I would not be denied my second century for England and

A thrilling climax to the past year – celebrating my seventh century during the Fifth Test against Australia in Sydney, January 2003.

Andrew Flintoff (*in red, front centre*) and Andy Caddick (*back centre*) lend a hand with Great Britain's Admiral's Cup team in Auckland Harbour, March 2002.

A self-inflicted jab with my bat causes some pain during the fourth one-day international against New Zealand in Auckland's Eden Park, February 2002.

Out for a duck – Ian Butler sends my bails flying in the First Test against New Zealand in Christchurch, March 2002.

Double celebration – Graham Thorpe (*left*) rejoices at his double hundred while Andrew Flintoff acknowledges his maiden Test century against the Kiwis in Christchurch.

Skipper Nasser Hussain cuts loose, rescuing England with a century in our first innings of the First Test in Christchurch.

On my way to a first Test hundred at Lord's in the opening Test against Sri Lanka, May 2002.

With arms aloft, Marcus Trescothick and I celebrate victory over Sri Lanka at Old Trafford, June 2002.

An exuberant Flintoff almost strangles me while Alex Tudor (*back left*) and Mark Butcher (*second right*) enjoy the winning feeling with Trescothick at Old Trafford.

Heavens above – John Crawley gives thanks for a century against India at Lord's in July 2002 while Parthiv Patel leads the applause.

You beauty – I lead the congratulations as Glamorgan pace ace Simon Jones celebrates the dismissal of India's Virender Sehwag at Lord's.

Pointing the finger of fate with Mark Butcher after I bowled Wasim Jaffer for my first-ever Test wicket, against India at Lord's.

Glancing the ball past a diving Rahul Dravid on my way to 197 at Trent Bridge in August 2002.

Over and out – wiping away the sweat as I walk off after my exhausting marathon at Trent Bridge in the Second Test against India, August 2002.

Sachin Tendulkar looks back in disbelief and keeper Alec Stewart prepares to celebrate the unlikely scorebook entry – Tendulkar bowled Vaughan at Trent Bridge.

Heads bowed, the England party remember Ben Hollioake during a minute's silence on the fourth morning of the Second Test against New Zealand at Wellington in March 2002.

eventually went on to make 115 before edging Perera to Sangakkara.

It was my best innings to date. To get a hundred at Lord's is always special, but to get one when you look as if you could lose a Test is particularly encouraging. Doing it when I had to keep my place, to give myself a boost and to shut some people up gave the innings an extra gloss. I did have a bit of help – Aravinda de Silva was bowling his off-spin and he did give me a couple to hit. I also pulled a few with a shot I had been working on for a while, because of its ability to disrupt a bowler's length and line. It is not a specific shot, just an instinctive one, and at that point I was starting to play it well.

I could not have asked for a better wicket on which to bat because it took all the pressure off. Scoring 179 in the match was a great start to the summer, but of more importance was the way I played. I felt in good nick – all the omens were good. The board in the home dressing room would now have my name on it as a centurion, another dream fulfilled and in only my second Test at Lord's.

We ended the day on 321 for 2, knowing that we had at least answered the criticism that had been levelled at us for three days and were now in a position to determine our own fate on a pitch that had shown few signs of deteriorating with age.

We had made a nonsense of the morning's headlines deriding us as a team in disarray and crisis and eventually declared on 529 for 5, leaving Sri Lanka needing 250 to win off seventeen overs – a bridge far too far even for a team of such rapid scorers.

England v Sri Lanka (1st npower Test Match)

At Lord's – 16, 17, 18, 19, 20 May 2002
Result: Match Drawn. Toss: Sri Lanka.

SRI LANKA	First innings		Second innings	
M.S. Atapattu	c Trescothick b Cork	185	c Butcher b Caddick	7
*S.T. Jayasuriya	run out (Vaughan/Stewart)	18		
+K.C. Sangakkara	c Flintoff b Hoggard	10	(2) not out	6
D.P.M.D. Jayawardene	c Trescothick b Flintoff	107	(3) not out	14
P.A. de Silva	c Stewart b Cork	88		
R.P. Arnold	c Trescothick b Hoggard	50		
H.P. Tillakaratne	not out	17		
W.P.U.J.C. Vaas	c Trescothick b Cork	6		
D.N.T. Zoysa	c Stewart b Flintoff	28		
T.C.B. Fernando	not out	6		
P.D.R.L. Perera				
Extras	(b 1, lb 13, w 1, nb 25)	40	(b 5, lb 2, nb 8)	15
TOTAL	(8 wickets dec, 169 overs)	555	(1 wicket, 13 overs)	42

Fall of wickets – 1st inns: 1–38 (Jayasuriya), 2–55 (Sangakkara), 3–261 (Jayawardene), 4–407 (Atapattu), 5–492 (Arnold), 6–492 (de Silva), 7–505 (Vaas), 8–540 (Zoysa).
Fall of wickets – 2nd inns: 1–16 (Atapattu).

England bowling:
1st innings: Caddick 38.3–6–135–0, Hoggard 39–4–160–2, Cork 35.3–11–93–3, Flintoff 39–8–101–2, Butcher 3–0–17–0, Vaughan 14–2–35–0.
2nd innings: Caddick 7–2–10–1, Flintoff 5–0–18–0, Hoggard 1–0–7–0.

ENGLAND	First innings		Second innings (follow on)	
M.E. Trescothick	c Jayasuriya b Zoysa	13	lbw b Zoysa	76
M.P. Vaughan	c Zoysa b Perera	64	c Sangakkara b Perera	115
M.A. Butcher	c Jayawardene b Fernando	17	run out (Vaas/Sangakkara)	105
*N. Hussain	c Sangakkara b Zoysa	57	lbw b Perera	68
G.P. Thorpe	lbw b Perera	27	c Fernando b de Silva	65
J.P. Crawley	c Sangakkara b Vaas	31	not out	41
+A.J. Stewart	run out (sub U.D.U. Chandana)	7	not out	26
A. Flintoff	c Sangakkara b Fernando	12		
D.G. Cork	c Sangakkara b Fernando	0		
A.R. Caddick	c Sangakkara b Perera	13		
M.J. Hoggard	not out	0		
Extras	(b 4, lb 7, w 9, nb 14)	34	(b 1, lb 9, w 1, nb 22)	33
TOTAL	(all out, 73.1 overs)	275	(5 wickets dec, 191 overs)	529

Fall of wickets – 1st inns: 1–17 (Trescothick), 2–43 (Butcher), 3–149 (Hussain), 4–203 (Vaughan), 5–203 (Thorpe), 6–214 (Stewart), 7–237 (Flintoff), 8–237 (Cork), 9–267 (Caddick), 10–275 (Crawley).
Fall of wickets – 2nd inns: 1–168 (Trescothick), 2–213 (Vaughan), 3–372 (Hussain), 4–432 (Butcher), 5–483 (Thorpe).

Sri Lanka bowling:
1st innings: Vaas 21.1–4–51–1, Zoysa 19–3–82–2, Fernando 22–5–83–3, Perera 11–0–48–3.
2nd innings: Vaas 44–8–113–0, Zoysa 34–6–84–1, Perera 30–4–90–2, de Silva 27–7–63–1, Fernando 26–1–96–0, Jayasuriya 25–6–66–0, Arnold 4–1–7–0, Tillakaratne 1–1–0–0.

Umpires: D.J. Harper (Australia) and S. Venkataraghavan (India).
TV Umpire: J.W. Lloyds (England).
Match referee: G.R. Viswanath (India).
Man-of-the-match: M.S. Atapattu (Sri Lanka).

I headed for Edgbaston and the second Test in confident mood, buoyed by my second international ton and a sense that my position in the team, if not entirely cemented, was based on far firmer foundations than it had been on the return from New Zealand.

Nasser won the toss for a change and his decision to invite Sri Lanka to bat in conditions more suited to bowling proved extremely accurate as we hustled them out for 162, despite losing the first session to rain. Muttiah Muralitharan was back in the Sri Lankan attack after missing the first Test and found the outside edge of my bat in the seven overs we had to face that first night, but Jayawardene proved as unreliable a first slip as Jayasuriya and spilled the chance. The life offered me the opportunity to go on and score my thousandth Test run – a chance I willingly accepted.

Trescothick and I went on our merry way the following morning before I was out sweeping to Muralitharan for 46. It is a shot in my repertoire and I had no qualms about playing it, even against a bowler of Murali's standard. Trescothick went on to record a big hundred, while the significant factor about Graham Thorpe's century that followed was that he went from 50 to a hundred batting with Hoggard. We try to drill it in as a team that it is so crucial that guys bat and do not throw their wickets away. The tail has to hang around for as long as they can because it is frustrating for a fielding team when the last few make a nuisance of themselves.

Thorpe was on 61 when Hoggard, the last man, arrived for what most thought would be a brief appearance. It was anything but that. He faced more than half of the 185 balls bowled to the pair, collecting 17 extremely valuable runs, while his partner advanced merrily to another century in a partnership of 91.

Sri Lanka needed 383 to make us bat again and we had two whole days to take the lead in the series. The Sri Lankans are not unlike Australia in one respect and that is they see no mountain too high. The last thing on their minds would have been to save the match through defence. It is not their style and their strokeplayers came to the fore at the start of their second innings.

We had early success, Hoggard dismissing both Jayasuriya and Sangakkara, leaving Sri Lanka 350 behind, but Atapattu and Jayawardene shared an unbroken century partnership, which would have added to their side's conviction that they could still escape defeat. The pair could not perform any more tricks on the resumption, however, and we had our guests at 225 for 4 at lunch, and 272 all out shortly afterwards.

The match was ours and we went to Old Trafford aiming to finish off the series. There is nothing worse than going into the final Test 1–0 up and losing. It had happened in Pakistan and New Zealand and we knew we had to end the run for several reasons, not least the psychological effect it has on a team.

Fortunately, it was a cracker of a pitch and everybody down the order contributed once Nasser had won the toss and elected to do the only sane thing. My own donation to the pot was 36 before Dilhara Fernando produced his slower ball and had me taken at mid-off. Trescothick and Butcher advanced our cause quickly with 126 in thirty-five overs, while on a rain-affected second day the Surrey man went on to a deserved century and we progressed to 377 for 6, the first ball of the day's play not having been bowled until after 2 p.m. We reached 500 the following morning, passing that figure for the third successive innings – an English record. Our total and the rain effectively put the match and the series beyond Sri Lanka's reach.

Our stack of runs and standard in the field forced them to follow on some 259 adrift, a brilliant performance considering the outstanding nature of the pitch and the fact that neither Caddick nor Gough played. For Hoggard, Flintoff, Tudor and Giles, four relatively inexperienced bowlers, to make them bat again was very impressive.

They managed to pass our total just after tea on the last day and it got to the stage where Atapattu had to come back to the crease, having injured a hand previously. He was just blocking it out. They were 49 in front with nine overs left, two of which would be lost to the change over.

Ashley Giles had the ball and I think Nasser Hussain would have looked at the scoreboard and said: 'We'll have another over and then call it a draw.' Giles had other ideas. He got Atapattu and then Murali first ball.

Trescothick and I raced off the pitch. In a situation like this it would not have been strange to see Flintoff or Stewart coming in first, but we did not give them a chance to change the order. I guess Nasser thought they're up for it, let them have a go. I was definitely in the mood to go in and have a thrash and win us a Test match. We needed 42 in six overs and posted our intentions in the first over when Vaas went for 8. When Fernando went for 16 in the next, we knew that victory was within our grasp. Murali could weave no magic and went for

10 and Fernando came back on to be hit for another 8. A leg bye off the fifth ball of the fifth over was enough to start the victory celebrations. It was a great game of cricket and to go out and be a free spirit with a licence to kill was a superb feeling, one that I would take with me into the series against India.

CHAPTER 4
INDIAN SUMMER

I never set myself specific goals for the simple reason that I consider it a pointless exercise. If you set a target and fail to reach it, it leaves you open to being considered a failure. Reach your goals and you wonder if you aimed too low or were not ambitious enough. It is a lose-lose situation, so all I try to do is ensure that my attitude and approach is spot on for every game. I know that if those two factors are in place, then at least I have the foundation for success. I do know that it is definitely true that if you are slack in either of those disciplines you will come unstuck. I suppose it is in all the psychology books about only trying to control the controllable and that may sound simple and somewhat silly, but it is dead right.

Nobody has ever pinned cricket down and I knew that the Indians would be a different proposition from the Sri Lankans, but I did feel in control of myself and happy with my game going into the new series. Certainly, I could not have asked for a better start to the summer.

The first match of a new challenge is always an exciting time and you are prey to a few more nerves than usual. I had never faced the Indians before at home and playing them at Lord's, despite my century there earlier in the season, induced a bit more tension than normal. With a big crowd in north London, nobody was keener than I to do better than I had against Sri Lanka.

I remember the wicket looking good, but there was moisture there and it was overcast as I made my way to the middle with a new partner, Mark Butcher, Trescothick having broken a thumb playing for Somerset. I batted for three hours, but unfortunately not in the middle. I had not had my pads on long before they were off again as left-arm quick Zaheer Khan got the fourth ball to nip back and I was trapped lbw for nought. In the previous match I had scored a hundred and now, as I walked off towards the practice nets, I realised that the next time I arrived at the crease I would be on a pair. Having to contemplate that fact for the next two days was not something I was particularly looking forward to.

Hussain and Butcher steadied the ship, but the latter was out just before lunch for 29 when we stood at 76 for 2 with honours even. Zaheer struck again just after lunch to get rid of Thorpe which meant that Nasser, a naturally aggressive batsman, had to remain uncharacteristically subdued, a fact emphasised by statistics showing that he needed 128 balls to reach 50. John Crawley batted fluently on his return to the team and by tea we had a respectable 177 on the board and Nasser was on 82.

Having scored a century against India at Lord's just ten days previously, Nasser was obviously in the mood to repeat the feat and did so off 192 balls. His partnership with Crawley was worth 145 before part-timer Sehwag came back to break it, but we still ended the day on 257 for 4 and in control. Of equal satisfaction was the magnificent ovation Alec Stewart received when he walked out for his hundred and nineteenth Test, an English record and testimony to just how well he has looked after himself over the years.

When Nasser finally went, just after passing 150, he had been at the crease for seven hours and had helped us to an impressive 487 – the partnership of 93 in eighteen overs between the skipper and Freddie Flintoff being a particularly ferocious and entertaining part of it. Our total was a commendable one, and we went about defending it in unconventional, but planned, fashion – Hoggard, Flintoff and White bowling wide of the off stump to a packed off side. It was a tactic that attracted the critics, but it was one that worked again and even better than before. We out-thought and out-fought them and a few of their batsmen lost patience and got out to wide balls, Tendulkar included. Far from being critical, I think the media should have given credit for the ploy because we bowled them out on a good wicket and achieved something we had never envisaged, a handy first-innings lead. To be honest, falling for 221 on that wicket was an affront to the groundsmen who had prepared it.

For two-and-a-half days very little else went through my head apart from the fact that I was on a pair next time I occupied the crease. It was a nerve-racking period because bagging 0–0 at Lord's is not something you want on your cv.

After my dismissal in the first innings, I went back to the dressing room and watched how I was out on television. I noticed something in my technique and went on the bowling machine in the nets for three hours, just working on grooving this one particular technique. It probably changed my game more than anything else at that stage. Nigel Stockhill, our physiologist, loaded ball after ball in the machine and the more that came at me, the better I started to feel.

I have always tended to move forward before the ball is delivered and then slightly back to get myself in a base, but I discovered that I was moving too far across my stumps – a natural thing that I see as a slight mistake rather than an error in technique. It just seemed that I was getting a bit closed off and not allowing myself the opportunity to get out of trouble if the ball came back as Zaheer's had done. If it did nip or swing back, I had to be in a position to be able to play the ball and not feel it thud into my pads and see the dreaded finger of fate raised against me. It was all a question of angles and I did not change anything drastically, just a couple of inches made all the difference. From that first-innings duck came something positive that allowed me to move on a step. The practice worked because in the second innings I went out and made another hundred and it was nice to see the Indians on the back foot.

Ganguly and gang were 266 behind, but I was somewhat relieved that Nasser did not enforce the follow on because I had already waited long enough to have the chance of repairing the first-innings damage. I lost three partners before the close of play, but John Crawley proved a valuable ally and at the end of the day the only question to be asked was when we would declare next day.

I have never found anything particularly significant in the term nervous nineties for I firmly believe that a batsman should treat every ball on its merits, be his score 9 or 90. I was on 93 when Anil Kumble came on and, having had a plan to use against him for the season, I decided it was time to bring it into operation. I had been working on a shot with Duncan Fletcher for a couple of years that involved going down the wicket and hitting the spinners over the top. Kumble had his men up at mid-off and mid-on, so I danced down the wicket and clipped one for four and did exactly the same with the next on the other side for 3.

Some critics said I had been a bit reckless in playing those shots in the nineties, but they will not convince me I was wrong. If you get out on 99 it is no big deal. In my book it's not the hundreds that count, but the big hundreds. There is no drastic difference between a 90 and a ton. Crawley also reached his century to herald the declaration and we ended up setting India a task beyond their capabilities – 568.

Of great excitement to me was the taking of my first Test wicket. Wasim Jaffer was the victim when he was on 50 and involved in a more than useful partnership. I somehow managed to get one to go up the hill and he snicked it straight to Nasser Hussain. It is a great feeling for a part-time bowler to get a wicket, especially since I do not get that much opportunity. I suppose the first one has to be the most memorable, but of course there was another I would soon value more. I consider myself a handy bowler, but had I wanted to be a frontliner I would have had to do a lot more work in that department. It is very difficult to be a first-class batsman and bowler and in the two previous years I had concentrated on my batting. The pressure has been taken off my bowling by treating it very much as a second string to my bow.

Of more interest than my bowling was the first appearance of Simon Jones, who was making his international debut after impressing everybody in the county game. We had heard a lot about him and his speed, but you never know how a player will react to all the media pressure and the presence of 30,000 people. Will the ball come out of my hand right is a commonly asked question among bowlers. We saw him first with the bat and what an impression he made. He smashed 30 off ten balls and that would have given him the confidence to go out and believe in himself when he was handed the ball.

The crowd was behind him from the off because they too knew that the new kid on the block propelled the ball at impressive speed. Simon did not disappoint them. He ambled in and then flung it down and I said to myself this lad's going to be a good 'un. He would have been relieved to take a wicket and then in the second innings he ripped straight through the defences of Virender Sehwag. One of the world's top batsmen had been done by pure speed. What a weapon for us to have, especially since he also showed an ability to find reverse swing as well.

We were playing well and knew the Indians were vulnerable when the ball swung, but we were also aware that when the wickets were better our visitors would prove more of a force. We had won the first battle by 170 runs, but there were three Tests of hard work ahead.

A Test win always has to be celebrated and this was no exception. Some celebrated more adventurously than others, although there is no great drinking culture in Test cricket today because you just cannot get away with it. The media attention

England v India (1st npower Test Match)

At Lord's – 25, 26, 27, 28, 29 July 2002
Result: England won by 170 runs. Toss: England.

ENGLAND	First innings		Second innings	
M.A. Butcher	c Jaffer b Kumble	29	lbw b Kumble	18
M.P. Vaughan	lbw b Khan	0	c Jaffer b Nehra	100
*N. Hussain	c Ratra b Agarkar	155	c Ratra b Agarkar	12
G.P. Thorpe	b Khan	4	c Ganguly b Kumble	1
J.P. Crawley	c Dravid b Sehwag	64	not out	100
+A.J. Stewart	lbw b Khan	19	(7) st Ratra b Kumble	33
A. Flintoff	c Ratra b Agarkar	59	(6) c Tendulkar b Nehra	7
C. White	st Ratra b Kumble	53	not out	6
A.F. Giles	b Nehra	19		
S.P. Jones	c Dravid b Kumble	44		
M.J. Hoggard	not out	10		
Extras	(b 11, lb 11, w 2, nb 7)	31	(b 5, lb 14, nb 5)	24
TOTAL	(all out, 142.2 overs)	487	(6 wickets dec, 64.4 overs)	301

Fall of wickets – 1st inns: 1–0 (Vaughan), 2–71 (Butcher), 3–78 (Thorpe), 4–223 (Crawley), 5–263 (Stewart), 6–356 (Flintoff), 7–357 (Hussain), 3–390 (Giles), 9–452 (Jones), 10–487 (White).
Fall of wickets – 2nd inns: 1–32 (Butcher), 2–65 (Hussain), 3–76 (Thorpe), 4–213 (Vaughan), 5–228 (Flintoff), 6–287 (Stewart).

India bowling:
1st innings: Nehra 30–4–101–1, Khan 36–13–90–3, Agarkar 21–3–98–2, Kumble 42.2–9–128–3, Ganguly 3–1–16–0, Sehwag 10–0–32–1.
2nd innings: Nehra 14–1–80–2, Khan 11–1–41–0, Kumble 24–1–84–3, Agarkar 11.4–1–53–1, Tendulkar 2–0–14–0, Sehwag 2–0–10–0.

INDIA	First innings		Second innings	
W. Jaffer	b Hoggard	1	c Hussain b Vaughan	53
V. Sehwag	b Giles	84	b Jones	27
R. Dravid	c Vaughan b Hoggard	46	b Giles	63
A. Nehra	lbw b Flintoff	0	(11) c Thorpe b White	19
S.R. Tendulkar	c Stewart b White	16	(4) b Hoggard	12
*S.C. Ganguly	c Vaughan b Flintoff	5	(5) lbw b Hoggard	0
V.V.S. Laxman	not out	43	(6) c Vaughan b Jones	74
+A. Ratra	c Stewart b Jones	1	(7) c Butcher b Hoggard	1
A.B. Agarkar	c Flintoff b Jones	2	(8) not out	109
A. Kumble	b White	0	(9) c & b Hoggard	15
Z. Khan	c Thorpe b Hoggard	3	(10) c Stewart b White	7
Extras	(b 4, lb 8, nb 8)	20	(b 4, lb 3, w 2, nb 8)	17
TOTAL	(all out, 81.5 overs)	221	(all out, 109.4 overs)	397

Fall of wickets – 1st inns: 1–2 (Jaffer), 2–128 (Sehwag), 3–130 (Nehra), 4–162 (Dravid), 5–168 (Tendulkar), 6–177 (Ganguly), 7–191 (Ratra), 8–196 (Agarkar), 9–209 (Kumble), 10–221 (Khan).
Fall of wickets – 2nd inns: 1–61 (Sehwag), 2–110 (Jaffer), 3–140 (Tendulkar), 4–140 (Ganguly), 5–165 (Dravid), 6–170 (Ratra), 7–296 (Laxman), 8–320 (Kumble), 9–334 (Khan), 10–397 (Nehra).

England bowling:
1st innings: Hoggard 16.5–4–33–3, Flintoff 19–9–22–2, Giles 9–1–47–1, Jones 21–2–61–2, White 16–3–46–?
2nd innings: Hoggard 24–7–87–4, Flintoff 17–2–87–0, White 16.4–2–61–2, Jones 17–1–68–2, Giles 29–7–75–1, Vaughan 6–2–12–1.

Umpires: R.E. Koertzen (South Africa) and R.B. Tiffin (Zimbabwe).
TV Umpire: P. Willey (England).
Match referee: M.J. Procter (South Africa).
Man-of-the-match: N. Hussain (England).

is greater than it has ever been, as is the attention to detail demanded of every international sportsman. There is no way you can harm your body because you know if you do you are letting your team-mates down. Players are generally much fitter nowadays and people's movement around the ground is faster. Everybody is expected to be in first-class physical condition and you only have to see how Alec Stewart works on his fitness to realise what you have to do to stay at the top.

But there are occasions when you have to let your hair down and a Test win is one of them. A chat about the game and a lot of mickey-taking goes down well with a few glasses of white wine. It is a good way of easing away the stress and pressure of what has gone before.

Unfortunately, Simon Jones had to withdraw with a side injury before the start of the second Test at Trent Bridge and that was a disappointment for us because we had all seen his potential. We were also missing Thorpe, who had new problems in his private life to be sorted out. He had not been fully focused during the first Test and we understood and sympathised with his decision.

It looked as if we would continue our dominance at the start when Hoggard took 2 for 17 off his first ten overs, but Virender Sehwag had other ideas, making a century, which enabled our guests to end the first day on 210 for 4. They added another 92, but lost 5 more wickets in the twenty-five overs bowled on a rain-ruined second day.

We faced a target of 357 when I walked out to bat with my new opening partner in the absence of Marcus Trescothick, Robert Key. The Kent batsman is a very funny lad with a dry sense of humour. I discovered just how chilled out he is when we made our way from the pavilion. I said to him: 'We'll try to get on top of them right from the off.' He just looked at me and said: 'Not a problem.' The wicket was not doing as much as I expected and I was about 20 not out at lunch as we chased their decent 300. Just after lunch, Harbhajan Singh came on and I asked Key if he had faced him before. 'Oh aye, oh aye,' he said. 'Stumped first ball.' It was a long time before I stopped laughing.

People talk about being in a zone, although I prefer to call it rhythm. Zone or rhythm, I do know that in the two hours between lunch and tea, I scored 90-odd runs, and it was probably the best I had played for England at that stage. Everything seemed to hit the middle of the bat and I felt on top of my game and extremely confident. Every loose ball was turned into a boundary. I could not see myself getting out. I was in so much control of myself and the situation that I felt I could hit down the ground, pull, cut, drive, hook and deal comfortably with the spinner. The crowd responded and everybody enjoyed themselves, apart from the Indians and their supporters. They even tried using an 8–1 field, but I still managed to find the gaps. Rarely if ever have I dominated an attack to such an extent and I was determined to enjoy the feeling, knowing that the next occasion might be a long way off.

The vein continued to be a productive one after tea until I reached 197, my highest Test score, and was caught behind. People wondered why I had tried to play such an expansive shot so close to 200. My answer was that I had played exactly the same throughout my innings and I was not going to change just because I was on 197. A double would have been fantastic, but I was not disappointed in any way to have got out when I did. I was simply delighted to have played the way I did to put England in a strong position.

Craig White weighed in with 90-odd, but Tendulkar, Dravid and Ganguly replied for the Indians with big knocks while we went after them with everything we had, including the pace of Steve Harmison, who looked the part on his debut. He had come in for the injured Simon Jones and, although a little nervous in the first innings, as we all are when playing for the first time, he showed his worth in India's second innings and troubled all their batsmen.

It was during that innings that I became a central figure in what was, as a bowler at least, my proudest moment in sport. Nasser Hussain tossed me the ball, along with a few simple and succinct words of advice. 'There's a big patch of rough outside the right-hander's off stump. Try to drop it there and let's see what happens,' said the captain.

I marked out my run and prepared to create mayhem and confusion. Well, that was the plan. I don't often get the chance to bamboozle the world's best batsman, Sachin Tendulkar, with my occasional off-spin, so this was an opportunity to relish.

My first two attempts were treated with utter disdain and the ball was smashed with consummate ease and power through extra cover for four. I was not downhearted because runs were not of any immediate importance; we just wanted Tendulkar's wicket. A third attempt in another over received the same treatment, but this time the ball seemed to come out of my hand with a much nicer feeling to it than before. I'll try that again but lob it up a bit more, I said to myself at the start of my run-up.

I propelled the ball on a slightly higher trajectory and from the second it left my hand, I knew it was going somewhere very close to, if not exactly in the middle of, the patch I was aiming for. I saw Tendulkar come out for a big, expansive drive and then the ball pitched. The next thing I saw was Stewart with his hands in the air and all of a sudden the weirdest sensation I have ever experienced on a cricket field engulfed me. Had this happened? Had I actually done this? Please tell me I'm not dreaming. Then it sank in that the scorebook forever, and all the following morning's newspapers, would record something I could never have imagined – Sachin Tendulkar, bowled Michael Vaughan.

The scoreboard offered its confirmation and I set off on one of the most elaborate celebrations ever seen on a cricket pitch from Bangalore to Brisbane or Lord's to Lahore. I just ran and ran towards backward point and I really did not want to stop. I felt like retiring then and there. Tendulkar bowled Vaughan – what else is there left in the game? I had gone through the defences of the best batsman in the world and here I was at Trent Bridge, in the middle of a Test against India, high-fiving all my colleagues because I had just skittled the great man. Nasser, Alec and all the others could not contain themselves. However, it was not spontaneous applause they broke into, but impulsive laughter – they could not believe it either.

But it did happen and I have the ball and the stump it hit for proof – both signed by the little genius himself, which he did when we talked about this unlikeliest of sporting occurrences after the final Test at The Oval.

Just as important as the fact that I had actually bowled Tendulkar was the manner in which I had done it. It was exactly the ball I wanted to deliver – not something I had ever before been able to do to order, such occurrences usually being a bit of a fluke. Unfortunately, I did not bowl as well as I would have liked after that, although I did get another wicket. I seemed to lose momentum, but I could not complain. Collectively, had we bowled better in the first innings we could have won the match. It was an opportunity missed to go 2–0 up and I hoped we would not regret it later. The man-of-the-match award that came my way was a consolation. Many players say honours like that have little significance, but they do to me. I think they are important because if you get one it means you have had a great game and it is nice to sit in the dressing room afterwards knowing that you have performed very well.

And so to my home ground, where I really did fancy us on the Headingley wicket. If a seamer bowls well there, he normally gets a bit of swing and uneven bounce, especially in the first day and a half. Then when the wicket starts to crack up, the bounce is even more unpredictable. When you bat first, runs are not as important as survival. It is essential to be there at the end of the first day and not to be out before halfway through the second.

Having won the toss, it was a courageous decision by Indian skipper Sourav Ganguly to bat on an overcast morning and with enough in the pitch to encourage the seamers. Rahul Dravid's patience on that first day was outstanding, although he was helped by our bowlers not operating as well as they can. He played and missed a few times, but he hung around and milked

England v India (2nd npower Test Match)

At Nottingham – 8, 9, 10, 11, 12 August 2002
Result: Match drawn. Toss: India.

INDIA	First innings		Second innings	
W. Jaffer	b Hoggard	0	(2) lbw b Flintoff	5
V. Sehwag	b White	106	(1) lbw b Hoggard	0
R. Dravid	c Key b Hoggard	13	lbw b Cork	115
S.R. Tendulkar	b Cork	34	b Vaughan	92
*S.C. Ganguly	c Stewart b Hoggard	68	b Harmison	99
V.V.S. Laxman	c Key b Flintoff	22	c White b Cork	14
A.B. Agarkar	c Butcher b Harmison	34	lbw b Vaughan	32
+P.A. Patel	c Flintoff b Harmison	0	not out	19
Harbhajan Singh	c Hussain b Harmison	54	b Harmison	1
Z. Khan	not out	14	not out	14
A. Nehra	c Stewart b Hoggard	0		
Extras	(b 1, lb 8, w 2, nb 1)	12	(b 5, lb 12, w 4, nb 12)	33
TOTAL	(all out, 101.1 overs)	357	(8 wickets dec, 115 overs)	424

Fall of wickets – 1st inns: 1–6 (Jaffer), 2–34 (Dravid), 3–108 (Tendulkar), 4–179 (Sehwag), 5–218 (Laxman), 6–285 (Agarkar), 7–287 (Patel), 8–295 (Ganguly), 9–356 (Harbhajan Singh), 10–357 (Nehra).
Fall of wickets – 2nd inns: 1–0 (Sehwag), 2–11 (Jaffer), 3–174 (Tendulkar), 4–309 (Dravid), 5–339 (Laxman), 6–378 (Ganguly), 7–395 (Agarkar), 8–396 (Harbhajan Singh).

England bowling:
1st innings: Hoggard 35.1–10–105–4, Cork 11–3–45–1, Harmison 20–7–57–3, Flintoff 27–6–85–1, White 8–0–56–1.
2nd innings: Hoggard 23–0–109–1, Flintoff 22–2–95–1, Harmison 29–5–63–2, Cork 12–1–54–2, Vaughan 21–5–71–2, White 8–2–15–0.

ENGLAND	First innings	
R.W.T. Key	b Nehra	17
M.P. Vaughan	c Patel b Agarkar	197
M.A. Butcher	c Dravid b Harbhajan Singh	53
*N. Hussain	c Patel b Harbhajan Singh	3
J.P. Crawley	c Jaffer b Khan	22
+A.J. Stewart	b Khan	87
A. Flintoff	b Khan	33
C. White	not out	94
D.G. Cork	c Jaffer b Harbhajan Singh	31
M.J. Hoggard	c Dravid b Nehra	32
S.J. Harmison	c Jaffer b Agarkar	3
Extras	(b 9, lb 17, w 4, nb 15)	45
TOTAL	(all out, 144.5 overs)	617

Fall of wickets – 1st inns: 1–56 (Key), 2–221 (Butcher), 3–228 (Hussain), 4–272 (Crawley), 5–335 (Vaughan), 6–432 (Flintoff), 7–433 (Stewart), 8–493 (Cork), 9–596 (Hoggard), 10–617 (Harmison).

India bowling:
1st innings: Nehra 32–3–138–2, Khan 26–4–110–3, Agarkar 24.5–3–93–2, Harbhajan Singh 45–3–175–3, Ganguly 5–0–42–0, Tendulkar 6–0–15–0, Sehwag 6–1–18–0.

Umpires: R.E. Koertzen (South Africa) and R.B. Tiffin (Zimbabwe).
TV Umpire: J.W. Lloyds (England).
Match referee: C.H. Lloyd (West Indies).
Man-of-the-match: M.P. Vaughan (England).

our attack. His concentration and application on that track were nothing short of excellent.

At the back of our minds we also knew that Sachin Tendulkar had had four knocks against us and not really hurt us, so a big score was imminent and this was Yorkshire, his home turf so to speak, as he had played for the county. He got 193 in one of the best innings I have ever seen and hit us to all parts of the ground. Dravid's equally important knock was a gutsy, grind-them-down effort, while Sanjay Bangar got 68 in about the same number of overs – another significant effort given the unpredictability of the pitch.

They were in a strong position after the first day and I sensed we were up against it when we went out chasing a target of 429 just to save the follow on. To say that we needed to bat well was an understatement. Unfortunately, it was the last thing we did, although I was progressing nicely until chipping one to cover on 61. I had received fantastic support from my home crowd and it was disappointing not to get a ton for them. The manner of my dismissal was also regrettable, but that was the way I had been playing all summer and sometimes if you live by the sword you feel the pointed end now and again.

The Indians, and full marks for the way they exploited conditions that we should have been more used to than they were, enforced the follow on. Headingley wickets do not improve with age and this one was no exception. The gremlins surfaced from the wicket as soon as we started our second innings. Some balls reared up, others kept low, leaving the batsman's mind in constant turmoil.

It was not easy to bat out there and the Indians were very

aggressive in their approach and a few words were exchanged in the middle. I do not mind things like that at all because I think it makes a match more enjoyable when there is a bit of banter. They knew they could put us under pressure and, although I was not out there long enough to get involved with too many verbals, they did seem to be targeting Nasser. He loves it when people have a go at him. He just stands up to them and gives it back.

It is always interesting to bat with Nasser because, for whatever reason, it does seem to get heated when he is in the middle. It is quite entertaining and keeps you amused when you are at the other end. Sledging Nasser is counterproductive because it seems to concentrate his mind even more than usual, as the Indians discovered. His hundred was very special, but it could not save the game.

If we had hoped that Freddie Flintoff might have helped turn the balance of power with the bat we had not looked in the history books hard enough. In the last Test he had played at Headingly he had bagged a pair, and when he came out for the second innings this time he was hoping to improve on the big fat zero he had returned in the first. Unfortunately, it was not to be and although he was able to shrug off his disappointment with a laugh, his thoughts on the Headingley wicket made for x-certificate hearing. So we left Yorkshire all square in the series as we lost by an innings and 46 runs.

Back to back Tests are always hard on the body and mind. We finished on the Monday, travelled to London the following day and had to get ourselves up for the fourth Test starting at The Oval on the Thursday with the Indians having levelled the series. We knew we had to be ready because they would be coming at us with bayonets fixed. They would be aiming to pin us against the boundary walls, seeking to exploit the slightest chink in our recently dented armour.

Marcus Trescothick was back in the fold and was soon in the thick of it again as we won the toss and batted. We knew the first day would be crucial as we attempted to get back on track, but I never imagined scoring 182 not out in the day. Everything seemed as good as it had ever been and I particularly felt at ease against Kumble, using my feet and hitting him around the park quite a bit. It is a great feeling to be in that kind of form in front of a fantastic crowd, hearing the roars and chants as the ball disappears to all sections of the ground.

My hundred came at more than a run every two balls and was my fourth of the summer. I am not a great one for records and statistics, but it was interesting to note that no English batsman had hit four centuries in a summer since Graham Gooch in 1990 and that there were only four others on the all-time list – Herbert Sutcliffe, Don Bradman, Denis Compton and Allan Lamb being the others.

It had always been a dream of mine to bat through a complete day and to walk off with my bat raised high. I was absolutely shattered, surviving for much of the last session on the adrenalin rush that accompanied every new boundary. I was sweating rivers, badly needed a massage and was in even greater need of a shower. That was when I made my first real mistake of the day because when the coach asked if I wanted to do the media briefing I declined, saying I would do it the following day after I got out.

The media were not best pleased. I had just scored 182 not out and the quotes that their masters were demanding were not going to be available. I was naïve. I should have spoken to them, but their attack on Duncan Fletcher was unjustified. They said he had pulled me away from them, but that was a load of rubbish. It was my decision, born out of the feeling of being completely knackered and prompted by the need to get taped back together again – I was struggling with my knee and was going to have an operation immediately after the Test. But I should have spoken to them, especially after having done so well. There are not too many days like that and I was silly not to give them a few minutes.

A couple of early fours the next morning convinced me I was on my way to my first double hundred, but Zaheer Khan had other ideas. He produced a real corker that I edged to the keeper and I was on my way back. Everybody said I must have been disappointed at getting out on 197, but that was the last thing I was. My take was this: I was lucky I had not received that delivery when I was on nought.

The best feeling was the knowledge that I had put the team in a good position coming on the back of a lost Test. We had them under real pressure as they chased 515, but then Dravid, as only he can, propped up the middle order and helped himself to a double hundred. Throughout the series we had just not been able to get him out. We tried every tactic from seam to spin, bouncers to yorkers and he treated them in his own inimitable style as he led the side to within 7 runs of our total. There was never much doubt that the match and the series would end in a draw and so it proved, although the weather was the final arbitrator. At least Trescothick was back on his bike as he scored 50s in both innings, having not played for two months, and the way we handled the spinners was a testimony to the way Duncan Fletcher had coached us over the last three years. Massive improvements have been made in that direction and it has been mainly down to his advice.

Apart from 242 runs in the match, I also turned in figures of 2–36, claiming Ajit Agarkar with the same ball I had trapped Tendulkar with earlier in the series. The player-of-the-series award went to Dravid and I received our man-of-the-series prize. It was a great honour to have their coach select me. It had been a fantastic summer to date and one I had not envisaged at the start of it. To score four hundreds and so many runs was beyond my expectations and also a testimony to the way the wickets had been prepared by all the groundsmen. It had been up to me to cash in and it was very pleasing to have kept the till ringing.

England v India (4th npower Test Match)

At The Oval – 5, 6, 7, 8, 9 September 2002
Result: Match drawn. Toss: England.

ENGLAND	First innings		Second innings	
M.E. Trescothick	c Bangar b Khan	57	not out	58
M.P. Vaughan	c Ratra b Khan	195	not out	47
M.A. Butcher	c Dravid b Harbhajan Singh	54		
J.P. Crawley	lbw b Bangar	26		
*N. Hussain	c Laxman b Bangar	10		
+A.J. Stewart	c Ratra b Harbhajan Singh	23		
D.G. Cork	lbw b Harbhajan Singh	52		
A.J. Tudor	c Dravid b Harbhajan Singh	2		
A.F. Giles	c Dravid b Kumble	31		
A.R. Caddick	not out	14		
M.J. Hoggard	lbw b Harbhajan Singh	0		
Extras	(b 12, lb 31, w 1, nb 7)	51	(b 4, nb 5)	9
TOTAL	(all out, 155.4 overs)	515	(0 wickets, 28 overs)	114

Fall of wickets – 1st inns: 1–98 (Trescothick), 2–272 (Butcher), 3–349 (Vaughan), 4–367 (Crawley), 5–372 (Hussain), 6–434 (Stewart), 7–446 (Tudor), 8–477 (Cork), 9–514 (Giles), 10–515 (Hoggard).

India bowling:
1st innings: Khan 28–4–83–2, Agarkar 24–4–111–0, Bangar 24–8–48–2, Harbhajan Singh 38.4–6–115–5, Kumble 35–11–105–1, Ganguly 4–1–6–0, Tendulkar 2–0–4–0.
2nd innings: Khan 5–0–37–0, Bangar 2–0–6–0, Kumble 10–2–28–0, Harbhajan Singh 7–1–24–0, Agarkar 4–0–15–0.

INDIA	First innings	
S.B. Bangar	c Butcher b Hoggard	21
V. Sehwag	c Cork b Caddick	12
R. Dravid	run out (Giles/Stewart)	217
S.R. Tendulkar	lbw b Caddick	54
*S.C. Ganguly	c Stewart b Cork	51
V.V.S. Laxman	c Giles b Caddick	40
A.B. Agarkar	b Vaughan	31
+A. Ratra	c Butcher b Caddick	8
A. Kumble	c Hussain b Giles	7
Harbhajan Singh	b Giles	17
Z. Khan	not out	6
Extras	(b 10, lb 6, nb 28)	44
TOTAL	(all out, 170 overs)	508

Fall of wickets – 1st inns: 1–18 (Sehwag), 2–87 (Bangar), 3–178 (Tendulkar), 4–283 (Ganguly), 5–396 (Laxman), 6–465 (Agarkar), 7–473 (Dravid), 8–477 (Ratra), 9–493 (Kumble), 10–508 (Harbhajan Singh).

England bowling:
1st innings: Hoggard 25–2–97–1, Caddick 43–11–114–4, Giles 49–12–98–2, Tudor 19–2–80–0, Cork 22–5–67–1, Vaughan 12–1–36–1.

Umpires: E.A.R. de Silva (Sri Lanka) and D.L. Orchard (South Africa).
TV Umpire: N.A. Mallender (England).
Match referee: C.H. Lloyd (West Indies).
Man-of-the-match: R. Dravid (India).

CHAPTER 5
COUNTY LINE

I was ten years old and not quite certain which end of a bat to hold when my father Graham found himself being re-located through his job in the engineering world. He brought me, my mother Dee, and my younger brother David from Manchester to settle in Sheffield in the mid-eighties. My experience of the sport that would become my love and profession was extremely limited until we moved across the border. I used to watch my dad play for Worsley Cricket Club where he captained the thirds, and just messed around with the other kids, playing football and cricket on the sidelines, but with no idea that cricket would become my calling.

My brother, who was more into cricket than I was at that stage, started going to the local nets in Sheffield and shortly afterwards I joined him at Sheffield Collegiate, Abbeydale Park. The coach there, Jack Bethel, must have seen something, although for the life of me I have no idea what, and after my first net sent me for a Yorkshire Under 11 trial. A few months and only two matches afterwards, I was representing the county at that level. It was a huge shock to me, and an even bigger one for my parents, because they too were totally unaware that

I had any particular talent as a cricketer. I have played for the county ever since and hope to finish my days as a cricketer wearing the famous white rose.

I was also oblivious of red rose/white rose rivalries. I learned through school of the traditions between the two counties, but it is not until you play the big games that you realise how much the matches mean. The rivalry on the pitch is never more intense than when Yorkshire face Lancashire, but off it the two sets of players probably get on as well as any others, if not better. I am a good friend of Freddie Flintoff, Glen Chappel and Warren Hegg and also of ex-Lancashire and England star Neil Fair-brother now that he is involved with International Sports Man-agement, who look after my interests along with those of many of the world's best golfers, including Lee Westwood, Darren Clarke and Paul McGinley.

Never once have I had stick from the other Yorkshire lads about where I was born. That is possibly because when I joined the Academy it was alongside players I had been involved with at schools levels and they probably did not realise I was born outside the county. It was not until the media started writing about it that my origins became public.

Anybody with the slightest knowledge of Yorkshire cricket will realise that, particularly off the field and in the committee rooms, we never carry our shotguns over our shoulders when there is the remotest chance that we can shoot ourselves in the foot.

We had changed our luck in 2001 by winning the Championship for the first time in decades and a lot was expected of us in 2002 because we had not changed our team much at all – with one notable exception. Out of the side and the county went our captain, David Byas. It was a controversial move because not only did he leave, but he went straight over the border. Yorkshire diehards would have considered that an act of treason not too many follow ons ago. In my opinion, David Byas should still be involved with Yorkshire County Cricket Club. Throwing away his experience and giving him to Lancashire after what he gave as a player and captain was nothing short of criminal. He had it in him to continue to play, and he finally accepted Lancashire's offer, a decision anybody in his position would have taken. I felt at the time, and still do, that there would be only one loser when David walked out of the Headingley gates for the last time. Even if it was as senior professional rather than captain, his help and advice to the younger players would have been priceless.

When I came up through the ranks as a youngster, Martyn Moxon, who had retired as captain, filled that senior professional position and if you had any problems or needed to chat to somebody you went to him. I am sure David could have filled that role very comfortably and been a rock for the young players from the Academy or second team.

David is a strict disciplinarian and an honest guy. He had his differences with Darren Gough, but they were never evident when the two played in the same side. We would be kidding ourselves if we thought that every team did not have players who were not of the same mind. Brazil won the World Cup and I would bet you £1,000 to a grain of sand that not all their players get on well together off the pitch – but on it, they fight for one another until the job is done. People put their grievances to one side on the pitch and work for the collective cause and so it was with David and Darren.

Let's face it, Yorkies do have a history of falling out. I have been there for a decade now and it is sad when you hear about all the great players and look at their pictures on the walls and understand that many of them left the county with a bad taste and in a head of steam. I believe we need to show a little more respect to the guys coming towards the end of their careers, use their experience and not just throw it away.

Yorkshire's season of hope and expectation started badly . . . and gradually deteriorated. From the very first day I could sense that things were not as they should be. Not having any gear did not help. The marketing job had been given to a new guy who had promised the players things such as new cars and clothing deals, but they did not materialise when they should have done. People might think that that should not affect you on the pitch, but ask any professional sportsman and he will tell you that if he does not have the right equipment and does not look the part, everything changes – your attitude, your thinking and your luck.

Players were having to hunt for last year's kit, but most had given it away at the end of the season to kids or people in the street. We were turning up in different gear from one another. Only one word fully describes the start to the season on and off the pitch – shambolic.

Our Western Australian coach, Wayne Clarke, tried to put us in the right frame of mind, but there was so much nonsense happening off the pitch, the last thing players wanted to do was exactly what they were paid for. When we turned up for our first Sunday League away game we discovered that our kit had still not arrived and the tracksuits we were supposed to wear would have looked big on sumo wrestlers. We had no white balls to warm up with and took to the field in a worse state of dress and mind than if we were playing for a pub thirds after a lunchtime session on Tetley's. We won the match despite ourselves.

Many of the off-field activities contributed to the harm that was being done to Yorkshire cricket, and the guys who did not get the runs or the wickets that they had achieved the previous year will admit that they just did not play well enough. There was talk that under Australian Darren Lehmann discipline suffered, but I can assure you that the ship was run just as tightly as it had been under David Byas.

Despite the team's floundering fortunes and organisational problems, we saw no reason to alter our social habits from what they had been in our Championship-winning season. One of our off-the-field activities was a beard-growing competition – in hindsight, not the brightest move for a team hurtling towards relegation. We were all given a different kind of beard to grow in a week and the worst would have to pay a penalty.

Maybe it was the wrong thing to do when we were struggling, but captain Darren Lehmann and coach Wayne Clarke were determined we were going to act exactly as we had the year before when we had claimed the title amid all kinds of japes and mischievous activities. My particular beard was of the old-fashioned mutton chops variety as once sported by Godfrey

Evans, an excellent Kent and England wicket keeper in his day. I turned up for the first Test at Lord's and within two seconds of walking through the dressing-room door, Nasser Hussain and Duncan Fletcher both said: 'Get that off.' I had no intention of getting on the wrong side of them so I went immediately to the shower room to remove the offending facial hair.

Back at Yorkshire, the new kit arrived seven games into the season, the cars rolled up and discipline was tightened. It was no coincidence that with everything settled off the pitch, our form on it improved. Darren continued to score a sackful of runs and led the side very well indeed.

I had a feeling that the one-day side was beginning to click and we could be a force. Young players such as Gary Fellows, Tim Bresnan and Anthony McGrath were starting to understand the different demands of the game and their roles within the team, and I sensed that something good was going to come out of all the earlier troubles. The problems had not been helped by injuries to one or two of the bowlers, which meant others having to bowl more and consequently ending up jaded.

I remember the first one-day cup match was away to Northampton. We had been going through a particularly barren patch and we all knew that this competition was massive for us. We played proper cricket for a change and won quite convincingly – our reward a trip to Essex, who had already beaten us in the other one-day competition. We were undeterred and I felt that there was such a buzz about the team that we might just pull it off: a spirit that convinced me we would do well. Everybody thought the game was lost when I got out and Lehmann went early. We were 150 for 4 with twenty-four overs left chasing their 250. Our reservations were ill-founded because Fellows and McGrath played out of their skins and took us through for a fantastic win.

The sniff of north London was in our nostrils, but in keeping with the way our season had developed generally we still had to endure one of the biggest semi-final débâcles ever witnessed. The match against Surrey suffered three days of rain and the rules stated that in those circumstances there would be a bowl out. We were all preparing for it and had a competition among ourselves to see who would be our representatives. Then the club, Surrey and the ECB, probably mindful of the number of ticket sales generated by the match, decreed that the match would be rescheduled for another day.

There was further controversy even before a ball was bowled when Surrey objected to the wicket because they felt it had not been prepared properly. We were the home side and wanted to play on it, which is exactly what we did . . . and out of our skins to boot. The track really suited our bowlers and the ball swung and seamed to such an extent that we limited Surrey to less than 200. Whatever reservations Surrey had had about the wicket were not transmitted into our dressing room because Craig White and Matthew Wood smashed the visiting bowlers to all parts of Headingley and knocked the runs off on their own. And so to Lord's for the first time in fifteen years in this type of competition. The least we owed our supporters at that stage was a final at the home of cricket.

With Darren Lehmann away on international duty, we had

his compatriot Matthew Elliott as his replacement and neither he nor several of the other Yorkshire players had experienced anything like it. You could feel the excitement and electricity among the players as we practised on Friday, the start of a magical weekend as the white rose came out in full bloom. Marcus Trescothick was making his comeback for the final after his thumb injury so that added a little edge and I will always remember Elliott saying on the eve of the game: 'This is special, I could do something special.'

I said to him: 'I hope you're right because if one of the top three or four does something out of the ordinary, then I think we'll win the match easily.'

We walked out of the Maida Vale Marriott to the team dinner that night and soaked up the atmosphere created by our fans. It would be special.

There were between 10,000 and 15,000 Yorkshire supporters at Lord's and I doubt that they stopped cheering, singing and drinking throughout the most memorable of days. Somerset won the toss, batted and were going well at 40 without loss off six overs until Trescothick managed to cut one to me and I somehow clung on to it one-handed high over my head. He could not believe it because catching is not a strong point of mine. Indeed, there are those who believe it to be a distinct weakness. They may have some justification, but my rating soared with this particular effort and what a great feeling it was to pluck one out like that in front of a full house at Lord's. It gave us all a lift and the belief that this was going to be our day.

Nevertheless we knew that beating their 240 was a tough

ask and it looked even tougher when we were 30 for 3, but Elliott was inspired and I was assisting him in our climb towards respectability when I was adjudged lbw. Anthony McGrath passed me as I was going off and he was coming in and I just told him that if he batted for Elliott we would be there at the end. He did exactly that, finishing on 47 not out while Elliott hit one of the most majestic one-day innings I have ever seen, scoring 128 and winning the match with four overs to spare.

Trescothick has played some unbelievable one-day knocks, but that one of Elliott's took some beating. It was simply exceptional as he manipulated the gaps with ease and hit fours when he wanted to.

It was only afterwards in the bedlam that was our dressing room that a slightly chilling thought crossed my mind. An Australian had sculpted one of the classic limited-overs innings at Lord's, yet in his own country he was not considered good enough for an international contract. What on earth are we up against this winter when he can't get a game, I thought to myself. It must be some Aussie team. I would soon find out just how good.

We stayed until half past ten at night before meandering back to the hotel where the reception we received could not have been bettered had we just brought home the World Cup. The champagne flowed long into the night.

It was the only champagne moment in the season. I played just two Championship matches. I was disappointed to miss so many games, but international cricket does take its toll and you have to be very careful not to try to do too much. Duncan

Fletcher is very shrewd in the way he pulls players out of games to try to keep them fresh.

I have not exactly been injury-free either. Indeed, I have been prone to problems ever since joining England. You name it, my calves, hands, shoulders and knees have had it. My knees have been particularly troublesome and in 2002 it was my right one that needed attention. I felt something go during a one-day game for Yorkshire, but it was not until I had trouble sprinting with any conviction at Trent Bridge against the Indians that I knew time alone would not be a healer. A scan revealed a tear in the right cartilage and it was decided that once the series was over I would have an operation, which would keep me out of the ICC series in Sri Lanka, but ensure I would be fit to face the Aussies, my number one goal of the season, having missed the entire previous series against them. I hope to be injury-free from now on, but I do owe Sheffield specialist Derek Bickerstaff a big thank you. He and my knees meet regularly and nobody knows more about them.

I would love to have played more games for Yorkshire, but my body and mind tell me I have to rest now and again because it is impossible to be switched on all the time when you are answering the demands of cricket week in week out. I am still registered to Yorkshire, but England pay my wages and therefore have first call on when I play. Ultimately I want to play out my years at Yorkshire because I want to win more games and trophies for them. I just could not see myself playing for another county, but Yorkshire being Yorkshire, you never know. I might not have the option.

That is for the future. What occupied all my attention as I

prepared for more sun Down Under was the prospect of facing the best team in the world, definitely at this time and some would argue of all time.

CHAPTER 6
TAPPING TENDULKAR

The opportunity to sit down and chat with Sachin Tendulkar is something that has to be grasped and cherished whenever, if ever, it arises. It had not happened in India where he is idolised and followed to such an extent that I am sure it is sometimes difficult for even his wife to get near him. The man is a living legend and whenever he is in public, he can never escape the crowds flocking to see him. People camp by the gates of his house and bring their babies in the hope that he will come out and touch them. They see it as a blessing.

Sachin is such an idol that everybody wants a piece of him. In the sanctuary of the dressing room he is still surrounded by hordes of people. He has enough hassle in India without me troubling him, but after the home series I thought I might get the chance. If I did, it would not slip through my fingers. Players move freely in one another's dressing rooms when a series ends and I was not going to miss out again. Armed with the ball I had bowled him with at Trent Bridge and the stump it had hit, I went into the Indian quarters and he willingly signed both. They have since been mounted and I plan to put them on display at my parents' home.

Not only did I get Sachin's autograph, but also a precious half an hour of his time. It was an honour I fully appreciated and he talked openly about many things, including the discipline at which he is arguably the best in the world, batting. With one eye on the upcoming Ashes series I was particularly interested in anything he might say about the Australians. It made for fascinating listening. The advice he gave was extremely useful and also confirmed what I had been formulating as my own plan of attack for Glenn McGrath and co.

Sachin tapped into his memory bank and recalled an instance in an Australia–India match when McGrath had bowled seven maidens on the trot at him during one after-tea session. He felt that McGrath was an exceptional bowler, but batsmen had a tendency to treat him with too much respect, prompting a fairly negative approach. The next morning he had gone out and decided that attack was the best form of defence and elected to be more positive, to take the game to McGrath rather than the other way round. His reward was not only a big hundred, but also the knowledge that you have a better chance against McGrath by meeting him head on than by being tentative and too respectful. Sachin did not say there was a wrong way or a right way to play McGrath, but he did accentuate the power of positive play.

I listened to what Sachin had to say intently because opportunities like that may not arise more than once or twice in a career. What he said got me thinking and planning. If I was going to let McGrath, Jason Gillespie, Brett Lee and Andy Bichel believe that they could pin my ears to the sightscreens, that would put me on the back foot and they would think they had my number. I was not intending to be totally gung-ho, slash and bash, but to be nothing other than positive. I talked to Nasser Hussain and Alec Stewart about it and they agreed. They thought you had to be up front against the Aussies.

My research also revealed that the English batsmen who had done well against the Aussies – Ian Botham, David Gower and Graham Gooch, for instance – had done so by going after them whenever possible. I realised that Australia had the best attack in the world – after the quicks had peppered you at 90 mph, Shane Warne was waiting to spin his web – but I went there intending to take every scoring opportunity without being either rash or reckless. It was a policy that would serve me well.

On a slight tangent, another and more surprising thing came out of my trip into the Indian dressing room. I have spoken earlier about how Duncan Fletcher has been instrumental in changing my technique against spin, as he has with the approach of the entire England dressing room. It had not gone unnoticed among the visitors because no less a batsman than Rahul Dravid, who had scored three hundreds in the series and averaged over 50, was asking Nasser, Trescothick and me how we felt he should play certain spinners. It was a huge compliment to Fletcher because he had been the one who had taught us all we knew. Here was a great Indian batsman, who had grown up on dusty, spinning wickets, asking us for our opinion on how to play spin – flattery comes no higher.

Duncan Fletcher is not only an outstanding coach, but also a great talent spotter. Within a few minutes of watching a player, he will know whether or not he is capable of moving on to the next level. He saw Trescothick score 150 at the end of one championship summer and then demanded that the Somerset player be included on the A tour. Marcus had been facing the South African Jacques Kallis, who can be pretty quick, and every time the bowler dug one in short, Marcus pulled him out of the park. In Test cricket you have to be able to play the short ball and have all the back-foot shots. Trescothick has the lot. He had been almost ground down by playing county cricket all his life and just needed one little kick to get him on the international scene. That knock in front of Fletcher did it and he has not missed a game since.

Without doubt Fletcher has changed my approach to batting over the last three or four years and definitely for the better. He never stops helping, either. Although I scored a stack of runs throughout the summer, he was still giving me little tips and hints to help me score even more. When a player is scoring plenty, some coaches think everything is rosy and must be working well, yet I had spells when my touch was not that great, even though the scorebook registered a different story. Fletcher works on those times. As soon as you tell him you are out of synch, he will look at a video for just a few minutes and then come up with the perfect solution, whatever the problem may be.

Talk about staying on an even keel, I do not think Fletcher has ever wobbled in his life. When we win a Test match you never see him jumping up and down. He remains calm, just as he does when we get hammered. Not only is he a shrewd coach, but also an insightful tactician and when he speaks it is with authority and not for the sake of it. Every sentence has a reason and a purpose and the respect we have for him is shown in the fact that every time he says anything, we listen to it and take it in. I cannot thank him enough for all the work that he has put in for me, and I say that in the knowledge that the other lads are going to be unmerciful in the stick they will give me for actually having said it. It will be worth every dig because Duncan deserves the highest praise.

He and Nasser work very closely together, but they always leave room for input from every member of the squad. Tactics, game plan and opposition are discussed before every series and match. Captain and coach will have consulted the senior players before bringing their views and proposals to the entire team. Every member can say whatever he wants and put forward any suggestions or alternatives.

Nasser acts as chairman at these meetings and talks about our aims for the series and how we intend going about achieving them. Then he just says: 'I'll name the team in the morning.' He is also hands-on in the nets, where he talks to players and particularly about mental discipline. He is open to taking advice himself and if I spot some flaw in his technique he will take it on board. We are probably still not as good as some other teams in complimenting one another and helping one another out, but we are beginning to understand the importance of chatting among ourselves about techniques, different opposition bowlers and conditions generally. Each and every one of us has a vast amount of experience to help the common cause. Help like this is crucial in the improvement of everybody's game.

Nasser is an aggressive cricketer and when things do not go right on the field he lets us all know if he thinks a player is not pulling his weight. David Byas was exactly the same at Yorkshire, keeping the team on their toes. On the pitch, Nasser is under a lot of pressure as player and captain, so you have to learn to understand that, being an intense character, he will blow his top occasionally, and especially with our team because we are so volatile and unpredictable.

The Australian media picked up on this and also the fact that Yorkshire captain Darren Lehmann had probably had some influence on my development. Darren, who is Craig White's brother-in-law, is a player I admire because of his natural gifts and talents, and he has passed on a few tips over the years.

After I had returned from my first winter away, I was not scoring very quickly and wasting a lot of balls and Darren just said: 'Every time you hit the ball, look to run. Treat a four- or five-day game as you would a one-day match.' It was sound advice because it automatically makes you a more positive player and when I took that on board it was no coincidence that immediately afterwards I started to score more quickly. At Yorkshire, he always passed on good advice about how to play certain players and he has come in for some criticism from the Aussie press for what he has done to help us.

We admire Darren greatly at Yorkshire and I am sure South Australia feel exactly the same, while Aussie skipper Steve Waugh will often go to him for advice on tactics because he has a fantastic cricket brain. It was unfortunate that he found himself in trouble during 2002 over a racist slur attributed to him after he was out during a match against Sri Lanka. Unfortunately, Darren's words carried through the dressing-room door and he paid the penalty. There are certain players in our team, Nasser primarily, but also Andy Caddick surprisingly, who are definitely to be avoided when they get out, particularly if it has been a bad decision. You just do not want to be in the dressing room when they come in.

I do not think Darren lost the Yorkshire captaincy because of this incident; there had been a lot of talk about Anthony McGrath being groomed for the succession. Darren loved captaining Yorkshire, and was happy to play for the team, Australian commitments permitting, but he always felt that if there was a Yorkshire-born player who could do the job, he should have it.

The next thing on the agenda for me was the operation on my knee and afterwards, while the one-day team headed for Sri Lanka, I went to the Ryder Cup to watch them all tee-off that first morning at the Belfry. For me as a cricketer, there is nowhere like Lord's, but when we arrived at the Belfry I realised exactly why they consider the Ryder Cup the greatest competition in golf. I cannot think of any occasion in any other sport to match the incredible hush that descends when a player prepares to drive off and then the ear-piercing roar after the ball has been propelled down the fairway. Darren Clarke and Lee Westwood have told me there is nothing they do in their sport that compares to the feeling on that first tee. I can imagine the ball shrinks and the fairway narrows. I vividly remember Paul Azinger changing clubs and then changing back again several times before yanking a shot into the rough. Golf is a mental game and it certainly got to him that morning.

The rehabilitation from surgery did not go to plan, or as quickly as I had hoped, and I was not looking forward to twenty-four hours on the plane to Australia, especially since my knee still did not feel anything like 100 per cent. In fact, I thought it had gone again in our first warm-up session in Australia, but after you have had as many injuries as I have, when you feel a niggle, you think it is the end of the world. The physiotherapist recommended rest and work, but when it still did not get any better it was decided to see whether a scanner could detect anything. There was something there that should not have been – some sort of bruise had developed – but it was taken care of by a steroid jab, which did the trick.

Kirk Russell, our physio for Australia, had me in the pool at seven in the morning and seven at night, working me really hard to get me on the pitch. It was not as if I was the only one he had to deal with or worry about. Darren Gough, Freddie Flintoff and Steve Harmison were also having problems and, although Steve pulled through, the other two did not recover in time to take part in the Ashes. It was obvious from the minute we arrived in Australia that the two of them were not right. Gough had arrived in a state that was very close to struggling and Flintoff was not firing properly either. His body language was that of a player who feared the worst for the immediate future. It was a dispiriting blow to the squad and extremely tough to take; two of our most influential players would not be facing the best team in the world.

Leading up to the first Test, it was nip and tuck whether or not I would make it. If I was to figure, I had to play in the final warm-up game in Queensland and we came round to the opinion that although my knee was going to be sore, it should be all right to bat on and field. We fielded for a day and three-quarters and then I smashed a hundred, so I could move on to Brisbane in much better heart and with a century under my belt.

I believe it was all to the good that I missed the Sri Lanka tour at the end of our season and the early part of our stay in Australia because it meant that I was heading for the first Test fresh in mind and spirit. I had also decided not to over-prepare and changed my mind about taking a look at their bowlers through video analysis. To be honest, it seemed too daunting a task. Concentrate on your own game, I told myself, and play the ball that you face, not the guy who is propelling it at 90 mph in your direction. Keep things simple – eye on the ball, hit and look to run.

Before we arrived, we knew there would be key battles to be won if we were going to contest the series. My partnership with Trescothick was going to be crucial, as was that of Gough and Caddick with the ball, while the all-rounders contest could also be pivotal. Yet here we were on the eve of the first Test knowing that, with Gough and Flintoff out, we were alive in only one of those three departments. On the bonus side, Simon Jones was looking the part, bowling fast and swinging the ball both ways. As a team we were thinking hang on a minute, we've found something here because this lad's special. He had taken 5 against Western Australia and we were genuinely excited every time he got his hands on the ball. I have only come across a few players who let you know something is going to happen when they are involved. Simon is one.

Australia would also have their sultan of speed. Glenn McGrath is not called the world's best bowler without reason and I was looking forward to meeting the collision head on. It would turn into the sub-plot within the big picture.

The series was still a week away, but for me it started on the second day of our final warm-up game against Queensland. We were still fielding and there were very few places on the boundary rope that the ball had not hit. The home team were something like 400 for 2. I remember looking round and seeing Steve Waugh, wearing his Aussie outfit and walking close to the pitch. I wondered what was going on and then the entire Australian squad came out and walked the full perimeter of the ground. The official reason they were there was for their pre-Test press conference, but to me they were saying: 'Hey, look, you are being whipped by Queensland and not one of those guys is good enough to get in our Test team.' There they were, walking round the ground to the full applause of the spectators, reminding us who we were up against, as if we did not know. If they were trying to get on our backs I am not sure if it worked, but they were long gone before I made my big hundred.

One of several amazing things about Australians is just how open they are. When they are being interviewed or writing in their columns, they are not afraid of saying exactly how they feel. They tell it as it is and do not seem to be perturbed about the consequences.

It was about this time that McGrath did a huge double-page

spread in one of the newspapers. Just as when approaching the wicket, he held nothing back and was not afraid to toss in the occasional bouncer. When we arrived in Australia we knew that he would have a go somewhere along the line because he always targets one of the opposition. Tendulkar, Lara and Atherton have all come in focus and I had wondered if he would afford me a similar honour. I was not disappointed. He went through every single player in the England team, saying how he was going to bowl at them and itemising their strengths and weaknesses. The Aussies have supreme confidence in their own ability and he was open and honest about everyone. We all had a giggle about his comments, but one of them stood out more than any other to me – I would be his number one target.

I took it as a huge compliment because it proved to me just how far I had come in twelve months. The number one bowler in the world had targeted me when only a year previously I was averaging something like 25 in Test matches. Now here I was in Australia and Glenn McGrath was saying: 'Michael Vaughan is my main target.' I just thought, this is a bit of all right, not bad at all. I've been picked out by the best in the world. I knew then that the battle was on and it was going to be tough, but I was ready to face the challenge head on. McGrath called me a grinder who could bat for long periods of play, but who could be suspect to the short ball. It was my intention to alter his thinking.

I also remembered a conversation I had with Nasser after the last day of the Oval Test against India. We were in a coffee shop in Chelsea and he asked me how I felt I would go against

McGrath and co, what plan I had. 'I'm not going to die wondering,' I said. He just stared back and replied: 'Oh, right.' It was my intention to have a go in the knowledge that, even if I failed, I had tried. Nasser reminded me of our little chat a few days before the World Cup started, but by then we were operating on an entirely different playing field.

In Australia, it was a very nice feeling to be able to back up what I had set out to achieve. It was a continuation of my new approach to my job in the team – to focus all my thought processes on the technical and mental sides, to be deliberately positive without being reckless.

When we tour Australia, unlike when we host a series, there is not one easy game of cricket. They are all tough and I include the so-called warm-up games. The first game at Lilac Hill was billed as a festival occasion. The opposition included a couple of forty-year-olds among the Western Australia players. Some festival! There were 12,000 people packed into a small ground just outside Perth and the atmosphere is best described as hostile. Quite a few of the crowd had had a few sherbets too many and they were far from reluctant to let us know what they thought about us, England, our families, the Queen and anybody and anything else they wanted to vent their feelings about. We had known what to expect; Alec Stewart warned us before the game. After that first one-dayer, the collective feeling was that we were in for one hell of a tour. We were up against a nation that was geared to seeing their side do well.

It was even more intense against Queensland. With just twenty overs of the second of a three-day match left, they were still batting in their first innings and we had not been to the crease. They had no intention of giving us a game of cricket. They would keep us out in the field for as long as possible, nail us into the ground, try to bowl us out cheaply and really put us on the back foot for the first Test.

Perhaps it is a philosophy we should follow in England. What would be wrong in preparing wickets that do not suit the opposition, although in Australia's case that might be difficult. We could do more to get on the backs of visiting Test teams. We give it to them too easily, although I do have sympathy with the counties. We play so much cricket that they rest their best players for the touring side games. It is a pity because when the Aussies, for example, play Derbyshire, it is likely to be the second team being paraded. I feel we should do all we can to make these games more important.

The Aussies also have other allies that we cannot necessarily count on. The press Down Under is very much geared to highlighting any weakness in the opposition rather than giving a balanced view. In Perth, we had fielding practice for forty-five minutes and I would imagine the number of catches taken in that time would be 1,000 and no more than ten would have gone down. The next day the headline in the paper there was 'England Drop into Perth', together with three pictures of three different players spilling the ball. They were on our case straightaway and about as accurate as Darren Gough after fifteen pints. Anything we did in practice or off the pitch, any hint of the tiniest confrontation, they put a huge perspective on and tried to make out that we were not a unit. Everything done in the Australian media is geared towards national success and they try to get on your back just as much as the players facing you do. But I do have a huge respect for everything Australian in cricket terms and I am sure we could learn a great deal if we looked at the way the first-class game is run there.

As the first Test approached, I would be lying if I said team morale was not that bit lower because of Gough and Flintoff's absence. There was a lot of tension in the camp and I was more nervous than I have ever been in my career. I am nervous before every game, but this was different. My feelings bordered on apprehension, although I knew that as soon as I crossed the rope I would be fine and in the mood to enjoy the occasion.

We had done a lot of physical and mental preparation in getting ourselves up for the series, but still there was something missing. There was a definite nervousness about the entire team as it finally began to sink in just what we were about to face. Perhaps we had put ourselves under too much pressure. We went out there to win the Ashes back and I know we felt we could do it if we played to our potential. But we were playing against arguably the best team ever. That should have allowed us to say: 'We're playing the best, so let's just give it our best shot.' That would have taken the pressure off and let us enjoy the matches, fight, have a go and, if we turned out winners, then fantastic. No team had got near Australia for four years so it was a huge ask to go out there and say: 'We're going to beat you.'

Our press built us up by saying we could win it and having 12,000 supporters there prompted us to think about the wrong things rather than just to go out there and give it our best. We would quickly discover just how effective peashooters were against shotguns.

CHAPTER 7

SIZING IT UP
DOWN UNDER

Our preparation for the Ashes series was as intense and high profile as I had ever known. There was a huge media contingent and everything we did was highlighted, focused on and dissected in minute detail. Be it as a team or individuals, we were back page and front, centre spread and leader columns. If anybody coughed, it was an epidemic; if anybody laughed, we were taking things too lightly; and if we were quiet or poker-faced, we were expecting the worst. There was nothing that went unreported, of both a factual and fictitious nature.

One thing that did actually happen was a white rose reunion of all the Tykes – home-grown and imported – which our Yorkshire team-mate Darren Lehmann attended, along with Jason Gillespie, a familiar figure from his days playing club cricket up north. There was plenty of good-natured banter to illustrate just how well most sections of the two teams fraternise off the pitch. I stress off the pitch because on it the Aussies know only one way to play it – hard and in your face . . . and particularly in your ears.

Mine took a fearsome pounding in the pre-Test Queensland match. Even when I was finding the boundary with relative ease, the Aussies were more than willing to let me know that they were not particularly impressed with my batting. No doubt Glenn McGrath would be agreeing with them pretty soon. What the Aussies fail to grasp in my situation is that far from allowing all the sledging to get to me, it actually makes me all the more committed to that particular innings. The Aussie crowd is not slow in having its say, either. Boundary edge fielding can be entertaining, although they seem to love targeting Andy Caddick, probably because of his Kiwi connection.

We had the final team meeting the night before the game and went through their entire side and the tactics they were most likely to employ. The management and senior players contributed most, but the opportunity was there for anybody and everybody to have their say.

The thing about the Aussie bowling attack is that they have an ideal balance for any wicket at any stage of a match. They have McGrath who is Mr Consistent. He knows exactly where to bowl to any given player because he will have worked out his strengths and weaknesses and have a plan to suit with the fields he sets or the length he bowls, maybe having a man out on the hook for me, bringing one in for somebody else, or an extra gully or another slip or short leg, as well as bowling different lines to different players. It is almost as if he has a floppy disk on every player and slips it into his computer of a brain when the next opponent is twenty-two yards away. He automatically clicks into gear as the linchpin of the Australian attack.

In any game of cricket the first over is crucial and he is the ideal man to bowl it for them. This is particularly so in one-day matches because you always want to get off to the best possible start. You do not want to go for 10 in the first over so they generally lob the rock to McGrath to set the tone for the rest of the innings. More often than not he does it. He is not the fastest, averaging in the early eighties, but sometimes he produces a short one and you think sheesh, where's that come from? He has a fast one in his locker, but I think he realises that over a long day in the field he might need his energy in the afternoon, so conserves it unless he really feels like letting one go. He basically sits in and gnaws away at a batsman's resolve, but when he gets a wicket, or the team does, he generally goes up another couple of gears. You know he will bowl in good areas and you have to be very watchful because he can nip it both ways. He is not an outswinger or an inswinger; he has a bit of both in him and you have to be very careful. He is a very clever bowler who varies his pace to suit the circumstances more than any other player I know. He tries to get you on the back foot and keeps you thinking. It is always a challenge to face him. I got on top of him a little bit in the winter, but he had his days when he was on top of me, so it was always a good test to try to overcome.

At the other end, Gillespie is the perfect foil. In a five-day game, I can't imagine McGrath goes for more than 2.5 an over and the same for Gillespie, who is a bit quicker and skids it through the ball gathering pace off the wicket. The ball hits the bat a bit harder and he puts it in the same kind of areas. For an opening bowler, he is of a fuller length than many and bowls very few short balls, just now and again to keep you thinking. I think he is a fantastic bowler. McGrath and Gillespie in a five-day game are probably the perfect pair because they can bowl on any wicket. You put them on a really flat deck with the first twelve overs of the new ball and you can guarantee that they will get some kind of movement off the pitch. I think it is because they just hit the track so hard. There is no break in concentration when they are in tandem. The Aussies always have this big umbrella field in the slip cordon area and you think to yourself, there's a load of gaps, let's exploit them. But they never seem to put the ball on the end of your bat to whack, so you do have to take that little bit of a risk and maybe pull the length or try to move them away from their perfect line and length. If you just let them bowl at you, they will put it in the same area all day and give you nothing to hit. Sometimes you have to pull McGrath's and Gillespie's length ball and try to get them wondering where you are going to hit the ball, rather than thinking where am I going to bowl it? It's a different mindset. There is always a stage where you have to get the bowler a bit worried about what you are going to do, you cannot let them bowl and bowl and bowl.

Their back-up bowlers are good as well. Andy Bichel is a superb cricketer. Although he had played at Worcester, I did not know a great deal about him at the start of the tour, but I knew plenty more afterwards. He is a true professional who gives it his all, no matter the situation. It does not matter whether he has nought for 80 or 3 for 20 he will bowl exactly the same. He probably does not have the control of McGrath or Gillespie, but he hits the bat harder than you would think and things always happen when he has hold of the ball. Whether he is being smashed around or going through a team, things happen. What he did in the World Cup and in the Ashes showed just how much hard work he has put in over the years. He is as conscientious a cricketer as you can get and very handy with the bat as well. He got them out of a bit of the smelly stuff in the World Cup with the bat as well as the ball. He and Andrew Symonds were the two Australian players of the World Cup and yet when they arrived in South Africa, those might have been the two guys you would have said would not play many games.

A lot of Australians come into the team late. You do not get that many twenty-one or twenty-two-year-olds playing – probably the last were Ponting and Lee. All the rest seem to come in at twenty-five or twenty-six. They have a really good finishing school and they are made to wait for their chance.

I had faced one ball in county cricket from McGrath and he got me out. It was a Sunday League game. I went in about six and hooked him straight down square leg's throat. Shane Warne had claimed my scalp for Hampshire and Gillespie had got me out first ball in a one-day international. Although I had never faced Brett Lee, Bichel had got me out somewhere along the line. What a great record I had against them! They must have been quaking in their boots at the thought of what I might do.

Warne's record speaks for itself and when he is out of the side they do miss him. He comes at you even when he is not bowling, standing at first slip chirping away. He is a very psychological player and tries to get into a batsman's head, forever trying to talk players out. Not only that, but he tells you how he is going to get you out. Rather than speaking to the captain in a discreet manner he will make sure you can hear him. He is one of their best chirpers. He will say things like: 'Don't worry, he's going to hit one straight to gully in a minute.' Comments like that I can just laugh off, but with an inexperienced player it might work, because Warne is quite clever at it. I remember once in Adelaide, he was bowling at Nasser and said: 'I'm going to throw one up, and you'll drive and edge it.' Two overs later he lobbed one up and, sure enough, Nasser edged it, but just as Warne was about to celebrate and say told you so, Damien Martyn dropped the catch. Not all his plans follow the script.

One thing I do know as he serves a one-year suspension for taking a banned substance is that cricket needs him back playing.

If Shane Warne missed the World Cup because he took a drug that was not going to improve his performance or make him stronger and all it was going to do was speed up his healing process to get him to South Africa, I think he should have been allowed to take it. You want the best players playing in a major tournament and Shane Warne is the world's best spin bowler.

Every series Warne says he has new deliveries, new this, new that, but I think a lot of this is psychological. He has a great leg spinner and great control and a magnificent cricket brain. He knows what a batsman is thinking at any given time and what he intends to do. He can organise right fields and he knows, because of his experience, exactly the pace to bowl on certain wickets. His variation is not that different; although he says he has eight or so different balls, it is basically the same one. He has a googly he does not use much and a couple that skid on, particularly a backspinner that he got a lot of Pakistanis out with by dragging them across the stumps and then bowling it straight on skidding. They all played the same shot and were right in front of middle when it thudded into their pads, leaving the umpire an easy decision. Basically, Shane Warne has a great cricket brain and I think that is his key attribute now, coupled with the psychological edge he has over batsmen. How well you are going to do depends on how much you want to listen to him and worry about him, but he is great to face because he gives you respect. If you do well against him, he is not one to give you abuse. He will just say 'Shot' and after the game and your innings, he will come in and say 'Well played.'

If Warne is a chirper, McGrath definitely pops his beak into the same seed trough. He is into you all the time and can be quite abusive. I just think if you are getting the best players in the world – the McGraths and Warnes – to say things to you, you must be doing something right; if they are quiet and going about their business, you know they have things under control and are basically winning. If you can get them to react, you must be playing pretty well. If an individual comes at you, things just might be going in your favour, but if an entire team comes at you, then you know you are doing well.

They came at me hard for the first two Tests particularly, as they did quite a few other players, too. Just take it as a form of flattery is my philosophy. Some of McGrath's chirps are pretty pathetic, but others are quite good and amusing. It helps me settle and enjoy the contest.

Brett Lee is the key to the Australian future, particularly in the one-day game. They lob him the ball and he has a great action, bowling at tremendous pace and setting up their innings. McGrath is Steady Eddie at one end and then you have Lee racing in at the other with near 100 mph balls and now more control than ever, more often than not getting one or two wickets early. With McGrath getting his customary quick one, you are normally three down before you have started in the one-day game. It is a lot to catch up, but Lee does set the tone with his aggression. I know it has not always been the case, but unfortunately it has been when I have faced him. In the past some people have said that with Brett Lee you will be all right because, although he is fast, he does give you a lot to hit and you will score freely off him. I have not seen that so far because his action and control have been spot on. The World Cup proved that he is now up there with the best around.

Brett's statistics in the one-day game are great and they are going to be similar in the five-day game. He is their future. He has come on first change quite a bit, but he opened the bowling against us in Perth and flew in and got rid of a few. In Sydney he started again and he is definitely different with the new ball in hand. Not only is he the fastest, but also accurate now and that is a deadly combination. There are no free runs and he seems to know what he is doing. Allied to a shrewd cricket brain, he is a definite force and is only going to get better, unfortunately.

Stuart MacGill is a more attacking bowler than Warne, who on certain wickets will just sit in and create pressure at the other end by bowling maidens. I do not think MacGill has the control of Warne, but he probably spins it more, so will bowl a more attacking line that always gives the option of scoring off him. But he is also capable of delivering the unplayable ball because he spins it so much, and he has a very good googly that he hides well. We played him at Sydney and Melbourne where it spun and it was good to face him because of the challenge. I had a good chat with him after the Sydney Test and he said how much he had enjoyed bowling at me because it was a good contest. I have heard that he is a bit of a head case and there have been times in the past when he has lost it, but I think he just enjoys the game and talking about it. A few years before, he had bowled England out for fun in Sydney when it spun, and I think he was quite impressed at how much we had improved against spin – another pat on the back for Duncan Fletcher and the way he has set us up against such bowling. Five or six years ago, facing Warne or Murali or Saqlain or MacGill on a spinning pitch, England more often than not would have been bowled out for next to nothing.

Hogg got into the one-day squad because of Warne's suspension, having previously done well with the A side. He has been a revelation and is quite hard to pick, especially since he is new on the block and we haven't seen much of his left-arm spin. He is similar to MacGill in that he is very attacking, so will give you an opportunity to score. He is also a more than useful batsman and fields well, so he is an asset to their one-day side particularly. It looks as though they have found another who is going to be around for quite a while.

As for the batsmen, Matthew Hayden and Justin Langer set the tone for all openers around the world. Six or seven years ago, numbers one and two would go out there to see off the new ball and hold the fort till lunch without losing a wicket. The approach now is to go out to try to hit the shine off the ball. They have set that tone, the positive approach all the time. Trescothick and I have set out to do the same because that is the way we play the game. If it is there to be hit, that is what we do.

My approach in the past has been a bit more measured because I probably did not back myself as much. I was not as confident as I am now. I knew I had the shots, but I was scared of playing them in case it went wrong. Now it is totally different. I just play them. I always knew I would have to up the tempo from the first two Tests I played and back my ability a bit more. Wanting to be out there scoring runs, you enjoy the game more and you tend to do better, more often than not.

Langer is a short guy, a tough little bugger, mentally very strong and typically Australian, who really hits the ball hard. There were one or two occasions when some of our guys, myself included, had a few words with him on the pitch because we thought he was being a bit of a tit, particularly during the not out catch episode in Adelaide, but you have to admire the fierceness of his competitiveness. There were times during the winter when he was outscoring Hayden. They are a good foil for each other because Hayden is big and Langer small, so bowlers continually have to change the length and line they are bowling. Bowl slightly wide to Langer and he smashes you through the off side, and if you bowl straighter, he flicks you. For Hayden, you have to change the plan altogether. You have to bowl a little bit wider because he is so strong when it is straight. If Langer has a weakness it is that sometimes he gets across his stumps and is out lbw – not that either of the openers have many weaknesses. Our bowlers found it tough against them because they come at you so hard. Then Ricky Ponting trots out at three and is just as positive. He hits it hard, but his technique is pretty sound. No matter the situation, he wants to score all the time and you rarely if ever see him block out a maiden because he is such a dashing player. We want to get him out but, if there is any consolation when we don't, it is how entertaining he is to watch.

Damien Martyn can dominate and get after you. He has a very good technique. More often than not he is the one player who will occupy the crease, just bat and simply be happy to keep out there. All the rest seem to come out and give it a really good flay, although a controlled one. It took Martyn a while to get back in the Test side after being dropped, but in the last few years he has been prolific.

We knew Michael Bevan at Yorkshire and he is phenomenal. He churns runs out in whatever form of cricket he is playing. He could be a Test player quite easily but they have such an abundance of talent, he sometimes does not get a sniff and just plays in the one-day side. Without doubt, he is the best in the world at it because he times his innings brilliantly. Psychologically he is the hardest nut to crack because he seems to win games on his own with just a little bit of help from the other end. That really does take some doing, but it is no fluke because he must have done it twenty-five times in his career. He seems to know exactly when not to take a risk or when to chance his arm, and that is an art very few possess. He may get 5 off twenty-five balls and you think, hey, what's going on, but he knows exactly what he is doing. He has been in every situation, knows the plan to adopt and backs himself. He knows if he is there at the end, they will win . . . and more often than not it happens.

I had seen a lot of Steve Waugh on the television, but for the first four Tests he was a pale imitation of himself. He was really struggling and we stuck to our plan of bowling at him. We bowled straight and cut off his scoring options, not allowing him to get his hands to the ball. At Sydney, closing in on his ten-thousandth Test run, with talk of retirement, we thought surely even he cannot write a script like that, but he demolished us either side of the wicket. To watch him score his hundred off the last ball that Friday evening, to see their prime minister walk across the pitch to shake his hand, were moments I will never forget.

Waugh is obviously a good captain but, let's face it, he has a bloody good team to captain. It really does not matter who of the eleven goes out to toss the coin because the Australian team runs itself. They must have a good coach to keep them disciplined and controlled because the only weakness that could creep into their play is complacency. I am sure that is the only thing their coach works on.

As for Adam Gilchrist, all I can say is I would pay to watch him bat. When you are fielding and he comes out, you just think, oh, my God! He tries to have a go every ball and it is entertaining from the second he takes his guard. His strike rate must be phenomenal in both forms of the game. His technique is not fantastic, but he has an unbelievable eye. He hooks, pulls, drives, he's got the lot, and the cricket he plays involves a huge enjoyment factor on every occasion. He is a brilliant keeper too, plays hard, does not chirp too much and comes across as a regular guy. He is a true star in Australia and they stick his wing nuts on every advert – maybe they should use Caddick over here in the same way.

I have not played much against Symonds, but he seems a very good team player. He is a dangerous cricketer with a special talent who could have played for England, but he chose Australia, a decision that was justified when he picked up the World Cup. That moment was still a long way off as we prepared to face the five-day Australians at Brisbane for the first Test on 7 November.

Off to a flyer – Sachin Tendulkar pulls Alex Tudor through midwicket on his way to a big hundred for India against England at Headingley in August 2002.

Rahul Dravid's flashing blade has Robert Key taking defensive action and Ashley Giles looking on helplessly from the bowler's end at Headingley in the Third Test.

India's captain Sourav Ganguly makes a point to me at The Oval after I had been named Man of the Series.

Yorkshire's players celebrate their C & G one-day final win over Somerset at Lord's in August 2002.

Darren Gough shows the power and determination England missed Down Under during a practice session at Lord's.

Aussie Matthew Elliott cracks Andy Caddick for four during his match-winning knock for Yorkshire in the C & G final.

Two sugars please – Yorkshire and England all-rounder Anthony McGrath gets his message across in no uncertain fashion.

Yorkshire captain Darren Lehmann in reflective mood during the lunch break ahead of returning to Australia for the Ashes.

Above left: Getting in some catching practice with right knee heavily strapped before the Third Test against Australia in Perth, November 2002.

Above right: Crossing with Trescothick on his way to a century against Queensland during the final warm-up game before the First Test.

Left: The one that got away – dropping Matthew Hayden during the First Test in Brisbane, November 2002.

Matthew Hayden shows the full face of the bat and it's another boundary for the Aussie opener in the First Test.

World No.1 paceman Glenn McGrath celebrates first blood in our battle in Brisbane.

Down and out – Ashley Giles practises but his left wrist is broken and his tour is over prior to the Adelaide Test, November 2002.

Justin Langer manages a wry smile after the third umpire gives me not out during the Second Test in Adelaide.

Feeling the pain after taking one on the point of the shoulder from Aussie paceman Jason Gillespie during the Second Test.

Waiting for the verdict – the jury is still out on the question of Langer's catch.

Jason Gillespie can't stop me hitting the ball past him on my way to 177 in Adelaide.

Glenn McGrath, at full stretch, catches me off Shane Warne's bowling during England's second innings in Adelaide.

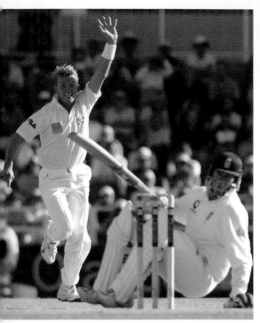

Aussie paceman Brett Lee celebrates the wicket of a fallen Trescothick during the Third Test in Perth, November 2002.

Bowler Lee and I look on as the bails go flying and Mark Butcher is run out in Perth.

Alex Tudor loses his feet and his helmet after being felled by a Brett Lee bouncer in Perth.

CHAPTER 8
BLITZED BY THE BEST

After the team meeting on the eve of the first day, everybody does his own thing. Some players have room service, but I prefer going to a restaurant with a few of the lads because I cannot stand sitting in a hotel bedroom staring at four walls and a television. I got back about 9.30 p.m., took in a bit of television and went to bed. It was no use losing sleep over the task ahead, formidable as it was.

I remember waking quite early and having breakfast by 7.20. Breakfast was mostly silent, unusually so, although there were a few of our supporters in the hotel wishing us well. I also recall feeling more nervous than when I had made my debut in the international arena against South Africa three years before. It had been a good year for me so far, but now I knew this was cricket at the very sharp end, against the world's best attack and I had virtually no experience against them. I was walking into the lions' den, but proudly wearing three lions on my chest and carrying a bat with plenty of runs still in it.

The only thing I had to take to the ground was my collection of bats because I always keep them in the room with me. Thanks to Gunn & Moore, I have a really good set and always take five on tour. The one I was using then lasted until the end of the Ashes series and helped me score five Test centuries. To say I was attached to it is an understatement. It has since been framed and signed and will no doubt find its way to my parents. There is a genuine sadness when a bat breaks and when this one went it prompted a longer period of mourning than usual. But, in Queensland, it still had plenty of work to do.

It was very quiet in the dressing room and the tension was almost visible. There is always an intensity leading up to games, but the atmosphere among the squad was really building. It rose daily and you could sense how players were becoming more and more switched on. The batsmen fiddled with their bats, making sure the handles were what they required and using tape to ensure the grip felt perfect, while others had a little weight taken out. The bowlers messed about with their studs. I am probably one of the messiest but also most relaxed.

It was a relief to get the practice gear on and go out to inspect the pitch – a wicket that became a huge talking point. It looked a dry one, but history had shown that it could do a bit on the first morning so it was difficult to determine whether or not to bat if we won the toss. The coin flipped down our side and Nasser elected to field – a decision that prompted a huge amount of debate bordering on controversy. I personally felt the pitch would do something and it did, but not exactly what I expected. It did not do much early on the first day, then eventually it cracked and became increasingly harder to bat on.

This was the first occasion I had been involved with the

national team when the national anthems were played. It really did hit home, not just the occasion, but the fact that we were thousands of miles away from England and representing our country. Looking down at the three lions and crest on my chest made the hair stand out on the back of my neck and served to increase the tension . . . as did the minute's silence observed for the victims of the Bali bombers.

Once the game got under way, the nerves disappeared and we went looking to make quick inroads. It was partially cloudy when Nasser called correctly, but the match was only a few overs old before the ground was covered in sunlight and it shone only on Australia. The Aussies came out and bashed us everywhere and our critics immediately said: 'What a stupid decision to field. Why didn't they bat?' Truth is, the majority of our team, not just Nasser, thought the ball and pitch would do a lot more than they did.

Andy Caddick and Matthew Hoggard are very good swing bowlers and we thought if we got into them early and took three or four wickets, the second and third days would be belters to bat on. Nasser gambled on bowling them out in a day and a session, leaving us the best of the wicket. It did not work out that way. Matthew Hayden and Justin Langer, after both being made to skip around the crease for a couple of overs, threw caution to the wind and went after us with a vengeance.

My first Ashes programme did not start at all well. The second ball of the day trickled to me at gully and I let it through my legs. People wrote, unfairly I thought, but I am biased, that the tone for the entire series was set by that one mistake. It gave a single to get Langer off the mark and it was not the best way to make a good impression or endear me to the captain.

Collectively, far worse was to happen as we found it impossible to bowl to Hayden. Wherever we set a field he would find gaps elsewhere. He smashed us everywhere around the ground and occasionally out of it. He arrived at the crease full of confidence and it quickly overflowed as he dominated our attack from ball one. It took us all of four overs to realise that there was not that much swing to be had and to understand the folly that it had been to field first.

Shorn of Gough and Flintoff, the last thing we needed was to lose another bowler, but within minutes of getting his first wicket in Australia, the prized one of Langer caught behind off one that seamed off the pitch, Simon Jones was on his way out of the series. He ran and dived for a ball, got his knee stuck in the ground and that was the end of his tour. I was closest to him at cover and, with my history of knee problems, knew the moment he went down that it was serious. We all sprinted over and he was in utter agony with what turned out to be a ruptured anterior knee ligament. The Aussie crowd showed typical consideration and concern. 'You weak English bastard, get up you poof,' they chorused. It was a terrific loss to us because at that stage he was looking pretty promising and had the Aussies worried by his pace. The Aussies were about 100–1 on a wicket offering nothing but assistance to them and nothing but heartache to us, and we had lost what was looking like our most lethal weapon.

They were plenty for 1 at lunch and as we retreated to the dressing room the general feeling was what have we done here?

There was a general hush, but Gough got us back on track with a typical wisecrack – when someone asked why he was called 'Rhino' his instant reply was 'because I'm as strong as an ox', and the spirit improved immediately. Unfortunately, after lunch so did the standard of Australian batting, and it had already been excellent.

Our strategy had been to pressure them and not even that worked until Hayden decided to send a skier to me at cover. Just like that first-over bloomer, the ball went straight through my fingers. When you drop a catch in front of one man and his whippet, you still want to dig a hole and sink straight into it, but to drop a dolly in Australia in front of the most abusive set of spectators I had ever encountered, I could not have done anything worse. I got plenty of gab at the Gabba as the crowd enjoyed themselves ridiculing me, and generally calling my parentage into question. My mum would have been quite miffed.

They hurled all the contempt in the considerable Aussie repertoire, and having to go and field on the boundary afterwards was not the most pleasant experience. Your confidence is not lifted when 10,000 Aussies are dishing out stick all day long. At least I escaped stick from my captain, colleagues and the Barmy Army. To them it seemed to be seen as just one more mistake in a day full of them.

The discomfiture we were receiving from behind the boundary rope, the Aussie batsmen were adding to out in the middle as they ran amok with the willow. Ricky Ponting, who would later succeed Steve Waugh as Australia's one-day captain, played a masterly innings, while Hayden confirmed his position as the world's number one-ranked batsman at the time with another blistering attack on the ball. When you are on a roll everything seems to go your way and, as well as my missed catch, he was also put down by Matthew Hoggard. Earlier, Simon Jones had suffered the misfortune of catching a Hayden skyer and then being helpless to prevent his momentum taking him over the boundary.

The agony only ended when we were on the team bus back to the hotel where a spot of tea was quickly followed by bed. Sweet dreams were not made of this as we faced the prospect of returning to the ground with the Aussies already on 364 and only two batsmen back in the dressing room. We went out for the second morning with a simple battle plan that involved nothing more than a collective aim of just putting them under as much pressure as possible.

Hayden fell three short of a double century after not adding many to his overnight score and then our spirits rose as Damien Martyn, Steve Waugh and Darren Lehmann, back in the side after almost four years, went relatively cheaply. Adam Gilchrist, who disfigures the ball every time he whacks it, was unable to alter its shape here and only Shane Warne of the lower order managed to offer any resistance. Ashley Giles and Craig White led our assault and their efforts proved just what can be gained from bowling quality line and length. The last 7 wickets went down for 128 and we could feel reasonably happy that we had restricted them to fewer than 500.

I went out to bat with Marcus Trescothick for a tricky little spell just before lunch. It was a walk we have taken together many times and I hope there will be many more and just as lucrative. I have developed a strong bond with Tres since our Under 19 and A team days together and we have a very good understanding. Testimony to that is the average of 121 we shared during the summer of 2002 at home.

Being left-handed makes him a nice foil and we aim to keep the field changing regularly. He is a very positive player who gives the ball a fearsome crack when he connects and he is also a very good judge of a single, particularly to the end he is running to. I know when he calls me it is going to be the right decision and hope he has equal confidence in my shout. The key to this is communication, a vital ingredient for any partnership, and although we are both positive players, we realise that to get on top of bowlers you do not necessarily have to hit them for fours all the time, but can achieve the same objective by rotating the strike.

My form throughout the previous summer with four centuries against Sri Lanka and India had taken my average to a respectable 47.5 and I was hoping to build on it rather than see it whittled down by McGrath. I knew there would be tough times when his immaculate line and length would restrict scoring opportunity, but remembering what Sachin Tendulkar had said, I was perfectly prepared to take the game to him if opportunity arose.

If there was one thing I knew to expect, particularly from McGrath, it was a verbal battering. I certainly got the ear-bashing bit right as McGrath stalked me right from the off, but I was able to show my intentions early because I was seeing the ball and feeling very well indeed. The sledging started straightaway, but I did not let it affect my concentration. I just said to him: 'I've got the bat, just get on with your bowling.'

We were off to a flyer and although I have the greatest respect for McGrath, chroniclers of the day's events were led to remark that I had not shown him any respect at all as I followed my intentions and took the game to him. I was not going to wait for him to get into a rhythm, which is when he can put the ball on a piece of the wicket as big as a postage stamp time after time. Actually, I attacked probably a little more than I had intended, but eventually he got one to nip back and I edged it behind. I remember walking off thinking hell, I could have got a big score there. I was disappointed at getting out for 33, but I had taken them on and had a go. A lot of people called it a ballsy effort to get after them, but I just called it positive.

The scoreboard did not look quite as intimidating as it had with 492 on it after the Australian first innings because we ended the second day with 158 runs for the loss of just my wicket.

You always know with the Aussies that if a side has a good couple of sessions against them, they will come back even harder. We needed to dig in and, if that was the intention of Trescothick and Butcher when they started the third day, they were soon to discover that our hosts were digging deeper into their resolve as well. Both were trapped by McGrath within five balls and once again we were up against it. The first wicket was McGrath's hundredth in Ashes history alone, highlighting just what a force he is.

Hussain and Crawley revived our hopes of at least getting within sniffing distance of the Aussie total with a partnership of 97 for the fourth wicket, but shortly after lunch the new ball arrived and with it the return of our old habits. Destroyer in chief was Jason Gillespie, often the under-sung hero of Australian causes, trapping Nasser with a real beauty and then forcing Alec Stewart to play on.

Crawley hung around as best he could and his 50 was the fourth of our innings, but he ran out of partners and was left unbeaten on 69. When four players claim a half-century, at least one, probably two, should go on, but none did and instead of being within winking distance we found ourselves waving at a team already 167 runs in the distance before their second innings started.

Australia do not believe in taking their time doing anything and they were soon after our attack in a bid to build a match-winning lead as quickly as possible. Langer was off at one-day pace with 22 from twenty-five balls, but then edged behind while Caddick also accounted for Ponting with an absolute corker that flew off a length, took the shoulder of the bat and nestled into the safe hands of Trescothick at first slip. Hayden did not notice any of the splits in the track and saw his team through to the end of play, destroying us once more. We tried everything to combat him, but nothing succeeded. Full marks to him because he is nothing short of great.

Langer and Ponting were our only successes and we ended the day with 8 wickets to collect and already 278 runs in arrears, knowing that we would be batting last on a pitch that was becoming more of a bowler's paradise with every ball.

They finished their second innings on 296 for 5, Hayden having scored 300 in the match. With their massive lead it was obvious we would have to play out of our skins to save the game. It would need a world record stand to set us up because we were chasing 464 to win. It proved a task too far. McGrath hit me on the pads with his third delivery and was lucky to get an lbw decision. I was sure the ball would have cleared the stumps, but the finger went up alongside the bowler's out-stretched arms. The only thing I could think of as I made the long walk was that McGrath had started the series saying he was going to make me his bunny rabbit and was 2–0 up on me already. I am sure he thought he had a psychological edge on me, but he was mistaken. I looked at the positives. I had played well in the first innings and been unfortunate in the second.

The rest of the team mirrored my misfortune as wicket fol-lowed wicket and our total of 70 was a disaster. The Aussies bowled well and took their catches, so at least we had not thrown our wickets away, but it is still difficult to wash away the embarrassment of being all out for such a low score.

We sat semi-dejected in the dressing room and realised just how good a team we were up against. We knew that to get to their level we were going to have to improve by 50 per cent. There was a lot of hard work to be done because they were not going to get any worse and might possibly get still better. Brett Lee could not even get in the side, for heaven's sake. Give them the scent and they go for the throat.

Back in the team room, over a case of wine, we had one of the funniest collective sessions of the trip. There was plenty of banter and I got no end of stick for the dolly catch I had dropped. I had put down a few in my career, but that was the most embarrassing and the opinion of my colleagues was that it warranted me being sent back to the Academy. But we were not totally dispirited and came to the opinion that, although we had been hammered, we were not that bad. It is quite easy to sulk when you have been beaten so comprehensively, but that evening we enjoyed one another's company.

The last thing you want to do the day after a Test match ends is to get hold of a bat and practise. The next Test was not for two weeks, so we needed to get away and relax for a while. We did this on the golf course and then travelled to Tasmania for a match against Australia A in Hobart – an important game because we wanted to get back in form. I scored 12 and 15 in the match, but I corrected the old problem of getting into a closed position with my foot movement, which had cropped up again in Brisbane. After the second innings I knew I was back on track. I felt good again and my movements were much better.

Only 27 on the scoreboard in the match did not bother me. Michael Atherton always used to say: 'Never waste your runs.' Whenever someone got 100 in a warm-up game he would say: 'Don't waste 'em, save 'em for the big games.' I looked back at the first Test in which I didn't get that many, and which I entered on the back of a big hundred. Athers was right so I did not consider I had failed in Hobart, just that I was due one round the corner. I had not wasted any.

We headed to Adelaide for the second Test starting 21 November without Freddie Flintoff and Darren Gough and the latest casualty, Simon Jones, but there was no point in feeling sorry for ourselves. This was fate playing its hand and the only thing we could do was relax and try to enjoy playing against the best team ever. If anything had come out of the first Test it was that we were no longer under the intense pressure placed on us, some of it by ourselves, going into the Brisbane match. Those who may have fancied us before the series started were now thinking more in terms of a whitewash and we were hoping that we might be able to turn that to our advantage.

It is good for morale and your own sanity that, even in times of adversity, you can still see the lighter side of life. We arrived in the nets for the practice session on the Tuesday before the Adelaide Test began on the Thursday to find 400 people waiting to watch. Somebody said: 'Aren't there a lot of people here?' to which Alec Stewart replied: 'It's because they've got five-day passes for the match and against us, the first day starts Tuesday.' Somebody else said: 'What do they want to watch us practise for?' and the reply came back: 'They know we get twenty minutes each and that's the most they ever get to see us bat.'

A sense of humour serves well in difficult times and the laughter those responses prompted showed that the spirit was still good. Unfortunately, the net session was not without its more serious moment with not only painful consequences for Ashley Giles, but also typical misfortune for the entire team. Giles, who had bowled beautifully on a flat track in the first Test, went in to bat and the crowd behind the net were urging Steve Harmison to bowl as fast as he could. 'Come on, Steve, let him have it,' they cried. He did and Ashley took a blow to the arm. He carried on batting, but when he came out he knew he had a problem and told me something was not right. He thought it might just be badly bruised, but x-rays showed a crack.

Ashley Giles is my biggest buddy in the team and I know he was desperate to play in Adelaide because of its history of favouring spinners. He was bowling well and then to be told he had a broken arm and was going home was a huge blow for him and the team. The way we were going it looked like we might struggle to have eleven fit players later in the tour. Gough, Flintoff, Jones and Giles, almost a complete attack, were all gone and, with Thorpe at home too, we had five key players missing for the second Test – mitigating circumstances should we be found guilty of failing to give the Aussies a proper game. If that was not enough, we also lost John Crawley to injury, so we were without more than half the side. This left a place for Kent's Robert Key to come in for his debut, having made a big hundred in the Hobart match.

Richard Dawson, who had not played since the first one-day game of the tour, would be playing just his fourth Test in Adelaide. I told him that there was no pressure on him and to enjoy the occasion because nobody would be expecting too much of him. I had no fears about my Yorkshire colleague because I knew he always had the right attitude, he possessed an astute cricketing brain and was more than capable of coping with the big occasion.

Even without most of our frontline bowlers, I still did not expect the outcome to be as clear cut as was being suggested. Our chances from outside the camp were assessed at slim and nil – and slim had just jumped into his car prior to driving out of town. The Australian supporters and their media were beginning to believe that their boys only had to turn up to beat us . . . and they could do it wearing civvies. With luck, the pressure would have moved on to Australian shoulders because of this. We just had to let Steve Waugh and his side know they were in a game.

Waugh is undoubtedly a great captain and king of the mind games. He loves nothing more than attacking the opposition's psyche by making macho gestures through field placings – seven-elevenths of his side occasionally forming a huge umbrella of a slip cordon. It can be an intimidating sight, but I intended turning it into a positive in my favour because, with so many waiting for nothing more than an edge, there would be plenty of open spaces in front of the wicket. I would enter the match with respect for Australia, but no fear.

The atmosphere at Adelaide is very Lord's-like. There are always plenty of marquees and it is very much a social occasion, the formal dinner we attended on the Tuesday evening, with a thousand guests, highlighting this. Looking at the wicket, we knew the toss was crucial and fortunately we won it. Unfortunately, I was unsure whether I would be able to take my place in the side.

Only a few of us realised that in the warm-up session before the game I had twisted my knee. I was struggling so badly that I honestly thought my match had ended before it had even started. Duncan Fletcher asked if I was fit and I was unable to answer, so he told me to get it strapped and then test it in the nets. By that time, Nasser was on his way to hand in the team-sheet and he was still not sure of my condition. I did a few sprints and I was still unsure myself, so physio Kirk Russell rang Nasser and told him. Nasser took the decision and left my name on the list. It was a name that would be on most people's lips all day and none more so than Justin Langer's.

Walking out to bat there were still a few doubts, but as soon as I got to the crease I felt my movement was good and after McGrath and Gillespie bowled well at the start, Andy Bichel came on and I pulled him for a six and then for another.

It was then that the biggest talking point of the day, and perhaps the series, occurred. I was on 19 and drove Bichel to cover where Langer dived low for a catch. In my own mind, the ball carried, but it happened so quickly that I decided I was in my rights to let the third umpire take a look. Trescothick came down the wicket and I asked him what he thought and he said he believed the ball had carried. Langer was 100 per cent sure that he had got two hands under it and the ball had not touched the ground. There was no quick decision and the longer it went on the more I was convinced it might go my way. Then I started to think the ball had touched the ground and when the decision went in my favour I just said to myself, fair enough. To say Langer was angry is a huge understatement. He was so red-faced I thought he had turned into something out of a giant packet of matches – this short strand of white with a big red blob on the end of it.

I was within my rights to stand and ask for a second opinion from the third umpire and I am convinced he and every one of the other twenty-one players on the pitch would have done exactly the same. For the rest of that morning session, Langer called me every name under the sun. That fired me up and I was determined to make him pay for it. I also told him during the height of the verbal abuse that a year earlier he had got away with something similar against the West Indies at the Sydney Cricket Ground.

Most of the Australians, I think, agreed that I was perfectly entitled to do what I had, but Langer would not let it drop and all day kept on giving me plenty. Shortly after my 'not out catch', Trescothick smashed one to Matthew Hayden in the gully, but it eluded his grasp and went for four. I am sure it did not help improve the state of mind of all the Aussies, and one in particular.

I was not the least bit surprised or concerned when Langer, as he was perfectly entitled to, did not clap my hundred. He was the least of few other problems I had that day as I got into a rhythm and played as well as I ever had. I was quickly into position and Shane Warne was not spinning it that much on the first day, enabling me to pick him off nicely. Gillespie bowled a really good spell after lunch that I saw off, crucially, I felt, because not only was he bowling a tight line, but he was also swinging the ball. For the rest of the day I felt in complete control on a smashing wicket.

McGrath made the first breakthrough when Trescothick played on off the bottom edge, but we were still handily placed at 94 for 1 at lunch. On the resumption, Robert Key was dreadfully unlucky when he drove Shane Warne into the shin of Ricky Ponting, who held on after a spectacular juggling act. I was in partnership with Nasser when a push to mid-off produced my fifth century in nine Tests, and that meant that I was averaging about a hundred a match for the last dozen.

I was just happy that I was putting the team in a good position as my ears continued to take a pounding from a Langer-led chorus. Approaching 150, they decided to give my upper body a workout and opted for the short stuff. I was ducking and weaving, but Gillespie arrowed one that I just could not avoid. It hit me on the shoulder harder than I had ever been hit before. The ball struck straight on the bone, my bat went up in the air and I was convinced serious damage had been done. I had never known a worse feeling, but it did make somebody happy. Langer was beside himself with joy as he let it be known he hoped it was nothing trivial that was contorting my face into such positions it must have looked as if I was taking part in the National Gurning Championships.

Maybe Langer would have been a little more reserved had he known that his words and antics were counter-productive. They only served to fire me up and make me concentrate even harder. I was able to continue after physio and marched on towards putting us in a great position in the match. Unfortunately, Bichel got the wicket Langer believed had been his earlier, in the last over of the day. I nicked one and even with 177 on the board I was absolutely gutted because I knew, had we gone in at 300-plus with only 3 down, we would have had a huge psychological advantage.

It was a weary walk back to the dressing room, but a very pleasant and unexpected surprise was delivered shortly afterwards. Jason Gillespie came in to shake my hand, pat me on the back and tell me: 'Well played.' He did not have to do it, but he made a special effort after all the drama and what had been said throughout the day. This was the first hand of friendship I had experienced from an Australian player on what had been one of the most remarkable days in my cricketing life.

There had been a lot of banter and stacks of abuse led by cheerleader Langer, well backed by some of his team-mates. For Jason to walk in and do that highlights the kind of guy he is. Not only is he a true gentleman, but a good man on the pitch, a great bowler who gives it everything.

I looked like something out of *Casualty* because I had a huge ice pack on my knee and one on my shoulder where Jason had hit me and I remember Duncan Fletcher turning to the lads and saying: 'That's what you've got to go through to score runs against this lot.' As I winced in pain, everybody laughed.

They have a board at the Adelaide Oval like the one at Lord's and they had already placed a sticker on it with my name and score. Looking at all the great names and seeing mine now added to the list was difficult to take in. The press conference that evening was predictable – 90 per cent of the questions being about Langer and the catch that never was. I just said what I felt at the time. I was within my rights to stand my ground, and the third umpire had been on my side.

Australia did not disappoint us the following day. We knew they would come back at us hard, but not quite as hard as they did. We resumed at 294 for 4 and were hoping for 450-plus, but Jason Gillespie and Shane Warne blasted and teased us out for the addition of a paltry 47 inside twenty-seven overs.

Gillespie's home ground proved a fruitful one for him as he caught the edge of Butcher's bat without addition to the over-night score, and then Craig White was caught by Andy Bichel at long leg trying to hook the pace man for six. Warne trapped Richard Dawson and Caddick and all hopes of a decent total vanished. When Gillespie came back for a second spell, he quickly accounted for the last two to finish with 4 for 10 on the day, 4 for 78 overall – emphasising the importance of keeping pegging away if at first you don't succeed.

Our bowlers could not achieve the same kind of break-through or restraint when Australia batted again. Hayden and Langer went on ball-assault from the off, but just when Hayden looked set for another massive score, he fell four short of his 50, and then Langer went, caught behind. Ponting and Martyn dispelled any hopes we may have had of restricting them to a reasonable total – Ponting unbeaten on 83 and Martyn two shy of a 50 when the last ball of the day was delivered. The pair eventually went on to record a partnership of 242, allowing Steve Waugh the opportunity to declare on 552 for 9, a lead of 210.

I was unable to lift my shoulder to throw, so I could not take my place in the field. The response from eleven Australians when I went out to bat was expected, typical and not particu-larly subtle. McGrath came down the wicket early to wish me a pleasant good morning, or I think that is what he was saying, and they went after me with plenty of short stuff, but by this time the wicket was really slow. Balls pitching halfway down the deck were exactly what a batsman wanted in those con-ditions so they would have been better off trying to lure me forward. Warne was coming round the wicket and hit a huge crater outside the leg stump. It was very tricky to negotiate and equally hard to score. Indeed, against the world's best spinner it was as hard a job as I have ever had against spin. I always try to score, but there just did not seem a way to do it. I could not find a plan or a way through the field.

Unfortunately, the Aussies found a way through our defences and picked up three more cheap wickets towards the end of the day, Trescothick, Butcher and Hussain being unable to add many more to those they had scored in the first innings.

There was a little bit of drizzle on that fourth day and we knew that not only was a win out of the question, but we would have to bat really well to get a draw.

Robert Key went in the second over when he pulled Andy Bichel down Darren Lehmann's throat at mid-wicket, but Alec Stewart came in for a typically tenacious knock, including his eight-thousandth Test run, which put him twelfth on the all-time list. My effort ended when I slog-swept Shane Warne and McGrath came round the boundary and took one of the best catches I have seen in my career, diving full length and parallel to the ground. The ball hit McGrath's left hand and flipped straight into his right. I was attempting to hit Warne into the George Giffen Stand, as I had on the opening day, but did not quite get the entire ball in the middle. It went up in the air, but I saw McGrath had lost sight of it and then Warne shouted to tell him where it was dropping. When it stuck I thought good catch mate, and walked off.

The rain that extended the lunch interval was neither heavy enough nor persistent enough to delay the inevitable too long. We were a lot more disappointed in being beaten in Adelaide than we had been in Brisbane because here we had been in such a good position on the first day and did not take advantage of it. Richard Dawson performed admirably on his Aussie debut and took wickets. It was good for him and his confidence, but we were missing key players and the Aussies were well on top

– playing with complete assurance, bowling well as a unit and scoring quickly. When you do that you have so much more time to bowl at the opposition.

I thought I had equalised in the batting-bowling match against McGrath, but he had caught me out so he probably felt he was still up in the contest. He always seems to play a part in every match, even if he is not taking wickets, and that catch was an indication. We try to say to one another: 'Stay in the game, do something,' because that is where the Aussies are so good. All of them seem to be part of the action all of the time.

It was handshake time at the end of the match and, although I did acknowledge Langer, the word coming back to our dressing room was that he still was not happy. I was told that a few of their guys were saying to him that he should let it lie now because he would have done exactly the same. He had also let it be known that he was not interested in socialising and that did not bother me in the slightest. I think if Justin Langer looks back he may consider he was a little childish. I know he is a passionate cricketer who plays with the Aussie badge on his heart, but although he felt it cost his side dearly, they still won the match whether I was out or not. We did not go into the Aussie dressing room after the match and, looking back, I think that was a mistake. We should have gone and talked through a few things.

There was plenty being talked about in the press. My own take on the third umpire is simple – for run outs they are fantastic. There is too much at stake for it not to be spot on and I do not think there has been one case where the third umpire has not been correct, at least in deciding whether or

Australia v England (2nd Test Match)

At Adelaide Oval – 21, 22, 23, 24 November 2002
Result: Australia won by an innings and 51 runs. Toss: England.

ENGLAND	First innings		Second innings	
M.E. Trescothick	b McGrath	35	lbw b Gillespie	0
M.P. Vaughan	c Warne b Bichel	177	c McGrath b Warne	41
R.W.T. Key	c Ponting b Warne	1	(5) c Lehmann b Bichel	1
*N. Hussain	c Gilchrist b Warne	47	b Bichel	10
M.A. Butcher	c Gilchrist b Gillespie	22	(3) lbw b McGrath	4
+A.J. Stewart	lbw b Gillespie	29	lbw b Warne	57
C. White	c Bichel b Gillespie	1	c sub (B. Lee) b McGrath	5
R.K.J. Dawson	lbw b Warne	6	c Gilchrist b McGrath	19
A.R. Caddick	b Warne	0	(11) not out	6
M.J. Hoggard	c Gilchrist b Gillespie	6	(9) b McGrath	1
S.J. Harmison	not out	3	(10) lbw b Warne	0
Extras	(lb 7, nb 8)	15	(b 3, lb 4, nb 8)	15
TOTAL	(all out, 115.5 overs)	342	(all out, 59.2 overs)	159

Fall of wickets – 1st inns: 1–88 (Trescothick), 2–106 (Key), 3–246 (Hussain), 4–295 (Vaughan), 5–295 (Butcher), 6–308 (White), 7–325 (Dawson), 8–325 (Caddick), 9–337 (Stewart), 10–342 (Hoggard).

Fall of wickets – 2nd inns: 1–5 (Trescothick), 2–17 (Butcher), 3–36 (Hussain), 4–40 (Key), 5–114 (Vaughan), 6–130 (White), 7–130 (Stewart), 8–132 (Hoggard), 9–134 (Harmison), 10–159 (Dawson).

Australia bowling:
1st innings: McGrath 30–11–77–1, Gillespie 26.5–8–78–4, Bichel 20–2–78–1, Warne 34–10–93–4, Waugh 5–1–9–0.
2nd innings: McGrath 17.2–6–41–4, Gillespie 12–1–44–1, Warne 25–7–36–3, Bichel 5–0–31–2.

AUSTRALIA	First innings	
J.L. Langer	c Stewart b Dawson	48
M.L. Hayden	c Caddick b White	46
R.T. Ponting	c Dawson b White	154
D.R. Martyn	c Hussain b Harmison	95
*S.R. Waugh	c Butcher b White	34
D.S. Lehmann	c sub (A. Flintoff) b White	5
+A.C. Gilchrist	c Stewart b Harmison	54
S.K. Warne	c & b Dawson	25
A.J. Bichel	b Hoggard	48
J.N. Gillespie	not out	0
G.D. McGrath		
Extras	(b 1, lb 17, w 7, nb 18)	43
TOTAL	(9 wickets dec, 139.2 overs)	552

Fall of wickets – 1st inns: 1–101 (Hayden), 2–114 (Langer), 3–356 (Martyn), 4–397 (Ponting), 5–414 (Lehmann), 6–423 (Waugh), 7–471 (Warne), 8–548 (Bichel), 9–552 (Gilchrist).

England bowling:
1st innings: Caddick 20–2–95–0, Hoggard 26–4–84–1, Harmison 28.2–8–106–2, White 28–2–106–4, Dawson 37–2–143–2.

Umpires: S.A. Bucknor (West Indies) and R.E. Koertzen (South Africa).
TV Umpire: S.J. Davis (Australia).
Match referee: Wasim Raja (Pakistan).
Man-of-the-match: R.T. Ponting (Australia).

not a player has made his ground. There have been one or two cases where the bails may have been broken before the ball was in hand, but in general, video replays do help with run outs.

Concerning catches, I was involved in the Adelaide one and I think it should go back now to players having the last say. Every replay taken to the third umpire seems to suggest it could have touched a blade of grass and therefore the decision goes with the batsmen. Maybe it should be that a batsman has to take the word of a fielder and that would bring more trust into the game. It could be tricky in tense situations, but either way it is hard because if you claim a catch and then a replay proves it did touch the ground you are going to be seen to be a complete fool. While the technology that we have is still in place, every batsman is going to stand his ground and wait for the replay. It also adds a bit for the crowd when they look at the screen and wait for an 'out' or 'not out' decision.

I know some people favour the use of the third umpire for lbw decisions, but I would never like to see that. There is no point in having umpires out there if you are going to refer everything, so I believe the third umpire should be used for run outs and everything else left to the integrity of the players. If you are 100 per cent sure you have taken a catch, then say so.

If you are going to claim catches when they have bounced well in front and get away with it, something will have to be done. You know if you have taken a catch and if you are the slightest bit doubtful you should say so and let the batsman have the benefit of the doubt. Nobody wants to look an idiot by making claims that are shown to be false.

Another debating point concerns premature celebrations. I

do not understand the fuss. If a guy has obviously snicked it, you are not going to just stand and wait for the finger to go up – he is out so you celebrate. If it is a bit doubtful, you stand there and appeal. For an obvious catch behind or at first slip you are bound to celebrate straightaway. Maybe the umpires should be a bit better if they think they are being intimidated or degraded. It is like a batsman saying: 'I don't want the bowler to appeal, it's putting me off.' It's all part of the game.

If we were a little deflated after going 2–0 down in the series, we had no time to ponder our position because we were heading for Perth and the second of the back-to-back Tests on 29 November. Our team was ever-changing. We had now lost Andy Caddick with a bad back, and Hoggard, one of the few still able to walk, was struggling to find swing and form. We had run out of fit bowlers and Alex Tudor was called up from the Academy and Chris Silverwood, another Yorkshire colleague of mine, was also drafted in.

We practised to get used to the bouncier conditions and tried to prepare for the match as best we could with one of the most inexperienced attacks England have ever fielded – Tudor, Silverwood, Harmison, White and Dawson.

We had a quick indication of just how well we were going to adapt because we had first use of the hard track. Aussie wicket keeper Adam Gilchrist was standing so far back he was almost a taxi-ride away, but the ball carried comfortably and I remember thinking that we were in for a tricky hour or two. McGrath hit his line perfectly and Brett Lee, who had been overlooked for the first two Tests, did not hold anything back. The rumours that he would be bowling really fast were not without foundation, and although all they tried to do was intimidate us, I knew what to expect. Lee was bowling extremely fast, faster than Pakistan's Shoaib Akhtar had bowled at me at Lord's, and that is fast. McGrath particularly was a real handful as he nipped the ball both ways. Trescothick went for 34 and Nasser cheaply but Key was looking comfortable and getting behind the ball well.

I was in a bit of a hole and not scoring, so I decided that I would have to try to put McGrath off his length and pull him, just as I had been trying to do all series. If he continued bowling the way he was, I would be out eventually on that kind of deck. But the first time I tried to pull him, I nicked one behind, which was a bit unlucky because if you edge one trying to pull, the ball normally goes flying over the slips. People might have thought it was a risky shot, but I had been playing to put him under pressure and to try to get on top.

We had thought that our luck with injuries could not get any worse, but it did. Within three overs of their innings starting, Silverwood's ankle gave way and he went off the park, while Harmison was struggling with his run-up. The Aussies played their shots, batted deep into the second day to establish a lead of 271 and left us with twenty overs to face.

The Freemantle Doctor came whistling in and Trescothick and I walked out expecting to face McGrath and Gillespie, but Steve Waugh gave the new rock to Brett Lee, downwind, and we knew he was going to generate something a little quicker than military medium. And so he did. In his second over he got one to lift to Trescothick. It came at him at Concorde speed and a catch spooned up off his glove. We were one down and

Lee was sniffing English blood. The smell did not leave him all session. Nightwatchman Richard Dawson came in and the first ball flew past his nose before he had much chance to move. The second would have gone straight through his chest, but he got a bit of a bat on it and it swerved past the slips for four. That spell of bowling was the fastest and most hostile I had ever experienced. Lee got absolutely everything right, egged on by a crowd baying for English corpses. Not only was it fast, but also swinging, a lethal combination, and I think everybody at the ground in both camps agreed they had never seen anything as quick . . . and by some distance. He had everything in his armoury and, putting it mildly, we were in a bit of bother.

Our suspicions were confirmed at the onset of the next day as two balls from Jason Gillespie kept low and then the next found some extra bounce and the edge of Dawson's bat en route to the safe hands of Steve Waugh.

I had been involved in a run out with Mark Butcher in the first innings when I called him then sent him back, but not in enough time. He went and I was not his favourite colleague at that moment. The tables were turned in the second innings when, without us having added to the score of the previous evening, and facing the twenty-third ball of the day, I hit one to widish cover and he called for a second when Lee slightly fumbled. When he recovered the ball, his throw was already on its way to Gilchrist when Butcher sent me back. Gilchrist quickly transferred it to the other end and I was stranded. It is a terrible way to get out and nobody means to do it, but it did look as if he had got his own back, and it was a press talking point afterwards.

Whether or not it unsettled Butcher I am not sure, but he was out lbw the next delivery and had a swing at the stumps to record his disappointment. We were 34 for 4 and lucky not to be for 5 when Nasser edged his first ball from Gillespie. It flew to the normally safe hands of Shane Warne, but the ball did not stick and the skipper stayed to offer some much needed resistance alongside Robert Key.

A measure of how difficult Australia were making it for us could be seen from the fact that after ten overs we had added just 5 runs to our overnight score and three more batsmen were back in the pavilion. It was only off the fifth ball of the thirty-second over that we recorded the first boundary of the innings. At least we had 78 on the board at lunch, but if that was the good news, consider the bad. We had 6 wickets left and still trailed by 193, and we had already lost two Tests by an innings. The portents were far from good.

The Aussie offensive did not let up and they seemed intent on bowling at Nasser's ribs and head, but this is the kind of assault the skipper rises to and his wicket was not going to be claimed easily. It looked as though we might even reach tea without the loss of another wicket, but Key's resistance was undone when McGrath trapped him lbw. His 23 had come off 106 balls – another indication of the difficulty of facing Australia's all-star attack.

With Hussain and Stewart at the crease we knew we had a great chance of at least making Australia strap their pads on again and we continued to ride our luck when Martyn put down a chance off Warne at slip. The captain would have had no quarrel if that ball had stuck, but he was dismayed when given out the very next ball. Playing forward and missing, he was given out caught behind and not impressed by umpire Rudi Koertzen's decision.

Craig White followed shortly afterwards, as did Alex Tudor, who was spared the long walk only because he was stretchered off after being felled by a fearsome Lee bouncer. It probably looked worse than it actually was, but people do tend to panic a bit at the sight of blood. He was being treated in the physio room when I went in and said: 'Don't worry, you'll only get a black eye.' Fortunately, he found it amusing.

There was nothing the least bit funny about losing the first three Tests and the Ashes. It was made all the harder to take because Australia is not the place for losers. Even the kids in the street smirk when they see you and occasionally you can hear them laughing behind your back, something I find extremely difficult to take. Looking back at the matches so far, the only good days we had had were the second day in Brisbane and the first in Adelaide. The Aussies had dominated every other day and session. I knew we were up against by far the best team I had ever faced. No wonder people were calling it the best ever.

So far, so bad. It could not have been a great deal worse because we could not hide from the fact that we had been battered and bruised throughout three one-sided matches. I really could not offer all the injuries as an excuse because, against this Aussie side, I am not sure our best eleven would have prospered enough to tame them. As an indication of just how many good players they have, I think an Aussie Thirds would be competitive at Test match level.

The press were still going on about our not visiting the Australian dressing room and the huge psychological barrier separating the two sides. They had a point but, as Nasser said: 'Talking to Glenn McGrath in the dressing room doesn't make you play him any better when he's twenty-two yards away.' Still, I felt we should have socialised, although it was not going to change the results.

However, throughout the series, despite our inability to cut the Aussies down to human size, the support we received was warming. In Perth, we all went out afterwards and clapped the fans and signed autographs. They gave us a great lift and told us not to get too down on ourselves because they realised just what we were up against. All they asked was that we competed to the best of our ability in the fourth and fifth Tests.

We relaxed and reminisced that night and it was impossible not to feel for the likes of Nasser and Alec Stewart and Andy Caddick. They might not get the chance to play against the Aussies again, yet throughout their time as England cricketers they had never got near to winning the Ashes. It was tough for all the players to be losing 3–0, but for them it was a particularly poignant moment because they knew they would never realise their dream. It was a situation I desperately hope to avoid in my career.

CHAPTER 9
CHRISTMAS CRACKER

My body needed a rest and the start of the VB one-day series after the first three Tests afforded that opportunity. It was decided that because of the workload and occasional grief from a suspect knee, I would miss the first series of matches.

It had been a punishing schedule. Actually, ridiculous is a more appropriate adjective to describe the itinerary of our winter. We played three Test matches, then the one-day guys came out and practised on their own before the first series. The guys who were not in the one-day side trained and tried to keep up their fitness levels for two-and-a-half weeks. They then came back for the Tests while the one-dayers had two-and-a-half weeks waiting for their next games. Still with me? I do not think there should ever be a programme like it again, but if there is, I certainly do not want to be involved.

Unless we are very careful, there is going to be burn out among players. I feel we are away from our families for too much time. It is not healthy for social, physical and family reasons to be away as much as we are. I am convinced the authorities are trying to cram too much cricket into too short a time just for the sake of television income.

Cricket is experiencing far too many injuries and even the Aussies, renowned for keeping the same side over a long period of time, lost several key players – McGrath, Warne, Gillespie – after Christmas. That is all due to the amount of cricket being played.

English players who play county cricket and then are away for the winter give their bodies a mighty pounding. Many feel exactly the same way as I do about it and there is a growing tendency for cricketers to choose one format of the game to specialise in. The schedule for the winter of 2002/03 was just too hard on the body to participate in both disciplines. To face what we were asked to face and then to go straight to the World Cup was not right. We should have been able to go home for at least two weeks, possibly more, so that we could re-charge our batteries, see our families and, not least, get away from one another. Steve Harmison had been away all winter and had a three-and-a-half-month old baby he had not seen. That is not good for your family life. A lot of players have little kids and they came out for Christmas and New Year for about four weeks. It was brilliant having them there, but to be at home with them would have been even better. My girlfriend Nichola came out to Melbourne, which was a great place to holiday in.

It was a strange feeling practising on Christmas morning at the MCG in preparation for the fourth Test, which began on Boxing Day. The wicket looked a present to bat on, particularly for those with first use of it. The toss was crucial, they won and elected to bat in front of 70,000 fans, including a lot of Brits. It was like the FA Cup final and Grand National rolled into one, a huge social occasion with plenty of drink taken and a lot of lairy Aussies not shy of telling any fieldsman close to the boundary exactly what they thought of Poms.

The Aussies made changes to their team for the match – leg-spinner Stuart MacGill came in for the injured Shane Warne, while Darren Lehmann had not been able to shake off a leg infection and was replaced by Martin Love, not only a fine batsman, but a very accomplished fielder. We also shuffled – Stewart's bruised hand meant James Foster would come in and keep wicket, and we opted for an extra batsman, Crawley replacing Alex Tudor, and Caddick came back to replace Chris Silverwood. The one unfortunate thing that did not change was Australia's dominance.

If there was any satisfaction in putting the Aussies under pressure and restricting them to 80/0 off twenty-eight overs, any confidence was knocked straight out of us after lunch. I have no idea what they ate during the interval, but when Hayden and Langer came back out they took us apart with all the subtlety of a wrecking ball. The crowd went wild and we went red – not knowing where to look or place a field. Langer had missed out for most of the tour, but he got a magnificent double hundred here which, despite our earlier differences and his childish attitude, I had no hesitation in applauding. Hayden was not quite as prolific, but did pass the 3,000 mark for Test runs. The pair also broke, more like shattered, the ground record for an opening partnership in an Ashes match. Monty Noble and Victor Trumper put on 126 in 1907, but Hayden and Langer squeezed past that mark. When their stand ended there were no fewer than 235 runs on the board. Two more wickets fell quickly, but there would be no landslide as Langer and Waugh continued a runfest that ended at stumps with Australia on 356 for 3.

Langer reached a career best 250 the following day while Waugh, under pressure from age and the critics, scored 77 and Love an unbeaten 62 before the declaration on 551 for 6.

It was still a great wicket to bat on when we came out, but I had only made 11 when McGrath got one to nick the inside edge. The ball ricocheted on to my pads and then the stumps. They were on top again and in those circumstances they are like a cat that has cornered a mouse. They keep flicking out paws until somewhere along the line the inevitable happens. Our middle order and tail performed well, but it was always likely that we would not avoid having to bat again, despite a gutsy 85 not out from White. All we could do was sit in the pavilion and wonder if they would enforce the follow on. For an opening batsman it is a nervy time because you have no idea what is going to happen. It was a situation of which Steve Waugh was well aware, the crafty old campaigner. Even though the series and Ashes were already won, he had no intention of releasing the stranglehold.

Tea was taken when the last wicket fell and that played into Waugh's hands because it gave him a few more minutes to dwell on the situation. He eventually came through and asked us to bat again. Far from being daunted or intimidated, I remember thinking that this was our chance. We were only about 220 behind and the opportunity was there to get a score. We also knew they would not want to chase too many on the last day.

My rhythm was there right from the start and I came in that evening with an unbeaten half century, although Trescothick and Butcher would be playing no further part in the match until we had to field again. We were only a hundred or so behind and still fighting. That night I went to the theatre with Nichola and it proved a very nice way to switch off from cricket and relax. We saw *Oliver*. Next morning I went out looking for more.

There is an honours board at the MCG that salutes centurions and I walked out wondering if I would have added my name by the end of play. Within an hour I had booked my place on it.

It was still one of the best wickets I had ever batted on and I was determined to feast on runs. I had never played better for England. It was becoming a feeling I had experienced regularly, not only during the series but also the previous summer. It was also a chance to face a new spinner in Stuart MacGill, but although he did get some turn it did not stop me hitting him around the park. McGrath was getting reverse swing but, similarly, it did not make any difference and I was able to get on top of Gillespie and Lee as well. There is no better feeling, at least on a cricket pitch. I was scoring freely and what a wonderful sensation when you are in control, especially when the opposition are wearing baggy green caps. I have rarely if ever had more pleasure raising my bat to acknowledge a century to add to those of Lord's, the Oval, Trent Bridge, Old Trafford and Adelaide. I think Lord's and the MCG are the most talked about grounds in world cricket and to have scored a century at both was a fantastic feeling.

I was well past a hundred by lunch and went out afterwards playing in exactly the same way. By the time I was on 145 we had come close to their total. I felt that if I was still there by the time that happened, we could maybe put on another 150–200 and have them under real pressure on the final day. Unfortunately, I got a bit cocky and played an average shot off MacGill to first slip where the extremely safe hands of Love did the rest. It was a terrible way to get out, cutting a ball that was too close, and although I did feel some satisfaction with my effort, it was still disappointing to get out the way I did. I was in such good form, I should have gone on to bigger and better things.

It was interesting to read afterwards how pleased MacGill had been to take my wicket and that he considered me to have a flawless temperament. 'He's certainly one of the more composed batsmen I've come across and he doesn't go into his shell either,' wrote MacGill. 'Getting him out will stand for me as a memorable moment in this Test match.' Praise indeed from an Aussie.

With my second hundred of the series and sixth of the year, I passed previous top-scorer Sachin Tendulkar's aggregate for 2002. The hundred also emphasised my attacking philosophy for the season for it came from just 153 balls. There were other useful knocks in the middle order, but the tail continued in usual fashion with 5 wickets falling in sixteen overs for the addition of just 45. At least 387 represented our biggest total of the series.

We finished 107 ahead, a ballsy effort, as they say, considering we were without seven key players. James Foster performed brilliantly in Stewart's place behind the sticks and got a few runs as well. He was one of many of our players who went up when Langer was smacked on the pads with the first ball of the two overs Australia had to face at the end of the fourth day. That near successful appeal at least gave our bowlers some encouragement for the following morning when battle would recommence with the Barmy Army in full voice.

The Army were not slow in reminding Brett Lee that there was a voice of opinion that suggested his action was not altogether pure, but my take on that is that he is a fast bowler who is a credit to the game. The pace he bowls at and his attitude do the game a lot of good. You know you are in a real challenge when you face him, but he gives credit when batsmen play well and does not sledge too much. He is never nasty, which is more than can be said for some of his colleagues, and I think he is great for the game ... and quite scary to face sometimes. Lee might be called a chucker now and again by the Barmy Army, but I am sure he loves fielding in front of them because it fires him up and he takes it all in good heart.

It was interesting to read, the following morning, one of the *Herald Sun* writers, Ron Reed, having a little dig at Langer for his criticism of the Barmy Army bringing Brett's bowling action into question.

'Justin Langer was getting a tad precious when he let fly at the Barmy Army for baiting Lee with constant calls of no ball, a reference to his action being under scrutiny,' wrote Reed. 'Langer called them a disgrace. But Justin, it was only barracking. You'll hear worse than that on any day of the footy at this, the people's stadium, as it bills itself. And plenty of people are pointing out it wasn't so long ago local fans were directing similar jibes at Sri Lanka's Muttiah Muralitharan.'

Lee had taken the stick in his stride and even responded positively when the Army asked for a wave when he was fielding close to them. I am not sure he was smiling quite as much when they asked him to repeat the gesture . . . but with a straight arm.

Arriving at the ground the following morning, I felt we were about 40 or 50 short, but we did what we had to do and got early wickets. Hayden hooked at a ball from Caddick and substitute fielder Alex Tudor took the catch; and after Ponting had looked as if he wanted to score all the necessary runs himself and in next to no time, he gloved behind a short ball from Steve Harmison. Just three balls later, Harmison got the faintest of tickles on Damien Martyn's bat and Australia were 58 for 3.

That gave us the faintest of chances and we might have got even closer but for a bizarre incident involving Steve Waugh. The fifth delivery went to our keeper and although television replays showed there was contact with the bat, nobody heard it at the time and so there was no appeal. Who knows what would have happened had we known he was out, but they eventually got the runs and went 4–0 up in the series. It was not getting any easier for them. This would be the first time in the series we had taken them to the fifth day and at least we had made a match of it.

We had fought manfully and put them under pressure and

Australia v England (4th Test Match)

At Melbourne Cricket Ground – 26, 27, 28, 29, 30 December 2002
Result: Australia won by 5 wickets. Toss: Australia.

AUSTRALIA	First innings		Second innings	
J.L. Langer	c Caddick b Dawson	250	lbw b Caddick	24
M.L. Hayden	c Crawley b Caddick	102	c sub (A. J. Tudor) b Caddick	1
R.T. Ponting	b White	21	c Foster b Harmison	30
D.R. Martyn	c Trescothick b White	17	c Foster b Harmison	0
*S.R. Waugh	c Foster b White	77	c Butcher b Caddick	14
M.L. Love	not out	62	not out	6
+A.C. Gilchrist	b Dawson	1	not out	10
B. Lee				
J.N. Gillespie				
S.C.G. MacGill				
G.D. McGrath				
Extras	(lb 11, w 5, nb 5)	21	(b 8, lb 5, nb 9)	22
TOTAL	(6 wickets dec, 146 overs)	551	(5 wickets, 23.1 overs)	107

Fall of wickets – 1st inns: 1–195 (Hayden), 2–235 (Ponting), 3–265 (Martyn), 4–394 (Waugh), 5–545 (Langer), 6–551 (Gilchrist).
Fall of wickets – 2nd inns: 1–8 (Hayden), 2–58 (Ponting), 3–58 (Martyn), 4–83 (Waugh), 5–90 (Langer).

England bowling:
1st innings: Caddick 36–6–126–1, Harmison 36–7–108–0, White 33–5–133–3, Dawson 28–1–121–2, Butcher 13–2–52–0.
2nd innings: Caddick 12–1–51–3, Harmison 11.1–1–43–2.

ENGLAND	First innings		Second innings (follow on)		
M.E. Trescothick	c Gilchrist b Lee	37		lbw b MacGill	37
M.P. Vaughan	b McGrath	11		c Love b MacGill	145
M.A. Butcher	lbw b Gillespie	25		c Love b Gillespie	6
*N. Hussain	c Hayden b MacGill	24		c & b McGrath	23
R.K.J. Dawson	c Love b MacGill	6	(9)	not out	15
R.W.T. Key	lbw b Lee	0	(5)	c Ponting b Gillespie	52
J.P. Crawley	c Langer b Gillespie	17	(6)	b Lee	33
C. White	not out	85	(7)	c Gilchrist b MacGill	21
+J.S. Foster	lbw b Waugh	19	(8)	c Love b MacGill	6
A.R. Caddick	b Gillespie	17		c Waugh b MacGill	10
S.J. Harmison	c Gilchrist b Gillespie	2		b Gillespie	7
Extras	(b 3, lb 10, nb 14)	27		(b 3, lb 21, w 2, nb 6)	32
TOTAL	(all out, 89.3 overs)	270		(all out, 120.4 overs)	387

Fall of wickets – 1st inns: 1–13 (Vaughan), 2–73 (Trescothick), 3–94 (Butcher), 4–111 (Dawson), 5–113 (Key), 6–118 (Hussain), 7–172 (Crawley), 8–227 (Foster), 9–264 (Caddick), 10–270 (Harmison).
Fall of wickets – 2nd inns: 1–67 (Trescothick), 2–89 (Butcher), 3–169 (Hussain), 4–236 (Vaughan), 5–287 (Key), 6–342 (Crawley), 7–342 (White), 8–356 (Foster), 9–378 (Caddick), 10–387 (Harmison).

Australia bowling:
1st innings: McGrath 16–5–41–1, Gillespie 16.3–7–25–4, MacGill 36–10–108–2, Lee 17–4–70–2, Waugh 4–0–13–1.
2nd innings: McGrath 19–5–44–1, Gillespie 24.4–6–71–3, MacGill 48–10–152–5, Lee 27–4–87–1, Waugh 2–0–9–0.

Umpires: D.L. Orchard (South Africa) and R.B. Tiffin (Zimbabwe).
TV Umpire: D.B. Hair (Australia).
Match referee: Wasim Raja (Pakistan).
Man-of-the-match: J.L. Langer (Australia).

that gave us a bit of hope as we headed for Sydney and the final Test. We were a happier dressing room knowing that we had competed for a few days. We had asked them more questions than we had managed to do in the previous three matches.

People were also asking questions about other issues. Although there was far less controversy surrounding this particular decision, the use of video replays to rule on contentious catches was highlighted again after Nasser was given not out when a catch by Jason Gillespie was referred to the third umpire. The Australian, in typical Aussie parlance, claimed the catch 'stood out like a dog's balls', but this would be the fourteenth successive time that the batsman had been given the benefit of the doubt. Justin Langer was still very much aware of the way the thirteenth referral had gone.

It prompted Malcolm Speed, head of the ICC, to suggest that flaws in the system might mean camera-assisted replays for catches would probably end within a year. The issue would be referred to the ICC's playing committee and then to individual boards. The last time it had been brought up, delegates voted 9–1 in favour of keeping the option – Australia's representative the only dissenting voice. He now had support, and powerful at that.

Speed indicated there was a growing feeling around the world that such matters would be best left to umpires because the third umpire was not always ideally placed to make an accurate decision due to shadows or poor angles. He felt that in future umpires should rule or fieldsmen be relied upon to say whether or not they had made a clean catch – an option highly favoured by West Indian bowling legend Michael Holding. I basically agree.

Speed also had something to say about the growing incidence of premature dismissal celebrations before umpires have given decisions. He said that he would be sending a missive of some urgency to all Test captains, umpires and match referees, showing his concern over the deteriorating standard of player behaviour. He was quoted as saying: 'Let's appeal, wait for the decision and then go into celebration. Nobody loses anything for that. What happens then is the game and the umpires get some respect.'

Neither issue was one that prompted much debate within the England camp after the match. At least I had levelled the one-on-one against McGrath by this point and may have been slightly ahead, but that did not mask the fact that we were facing a whitewash. Sydney would be the decider, but it was not to be. McGrath had been injured during the Melbourne game, probably through overwork, and would miss the conclusion. He had had a very long period in the field and picked up an injury, which is precisely what our bowlers have been up against for the last couple of years. The more you play the harder it gets. It's a tough job being a 'quick' and he was paying the price.

If we had had 8,000 supporters in Melbourne, there must have been 20,000 in Sydney. To hear them singing and chanting our names, getting stuck into the Aussies and behind us really fired us up. The Barmy Army are truly incredible. No matter how well or badly we have played they are always right behind us. As players, we are proud of them because, although they

like the odd beer or six, there is never any trouble from them.
And so we were all in good spirits as we headed for Sydney
... and some consolation.

CHAPTER 10
FIRST AT LAST

We were 4–0 down in the series, but far from deflated as our entourage of approaching ninety made its way to Sydney and some New Year's Eve celebrations before the final Test started on 2 January 2003. Sir Christopher Gent, chief executive of our sponsors Vodafone, had reserved the number one berth in the Harbour and we were regally entertained to a sit-down dinner followed by disco, and the chance to relax and have a welcome bit of fun. Vodafone are excellent sponsors and do look after us, especially their representative on tour, Jim Souter, who organises all the social events and the golf . . . we owe him plenty.

We also felt that we were in the debt of our wonderful supporters and knew there would be a record number of them at the SCG, despite the fact that the Ashes were already lost.

The one thing we had not had much trouble with for most of the series was winning the toss and here we elected to bat. It was the right decision, but Brett Lee decided to bowl as fast as he had since he returned to the side for the third Test, and he also swung the ball more than ever. It is never confidence-building when you play and miss, but when five out of six balls sail past the edge of the bat it can be downright embarrassing. Things had to change. They did. He got me out when I went chasing a wide swinger. So having scored 145 in my previous knock, I was now walking off with nought against my name on the second day of the New Year.

That 145 had brought me the most ever runs in a calendar year, and it was nice to know I was now top of a list that had once been led by Gooch, Gower and other big names. Also, to be leading run-scorer, ahead of Hayden, Tendulkar and Ponting, showed I must have played pretty well. Everybody was writing about whether I could do it again in 2003. I thought to myself that if my form continued it would be very special, but it would be hard to live up to what I had achieved in 2002. Walking off with a duck, I knew exactly what the media would be thinking. Is Vaughan a one-year wonder and was his success a mere flash in the pan?

While I was contemplating my nought, Mark Butcher, who had been struggling for form all series, went out and scored a fantastic hundred. Sydney wickets are not known for their durability so it is essential to get your runs posted early. That's exactly what Butcher did, backed by the skipper, who may have remembered that the only time he had led England to triumph over the Aussies was at Headingley in 2001 when Butcher again produced a magnificent hundred.

Here, the pair put on 166 for the third wicket on the way to us posting a respectable 264 for 5 on the opening day against a side finding out for the first time what we had experienced all series – just how difficult it is when shorn of key performers.

Australia were without McGrath and Warne, so here was our chance.

But with only 32 runs on the board and both Trescothick and I looking on from the dressing room, our followers must have wondered if we were capable of taking that opportunity. Indeed, Lee might have had another scalp the very next ball after claiming mine. Butcher must have been mightily relieved when umpire Russell Tiffin's finger stayed down following an lbw appeal that was probably audible across the water in New Zealand. Fortunately, Tiffin turned a deaf ear to the shout and, after surviving several early scares, Butcher went on to record one of his finest knocks.

Once Butcher passed 50 it seemed inevitable that he would make it to three figures and, sure enough, he had 124 on the board before being undone by the new ball. Crawley and Stewart held the middle order together after a threatened collapse and we ended the day feeling that we had credit in the bank for Brett Lee had really been a handful, primarily because of the distance he was swinging the ball.

I thought it was fantastic when Alec Stewart went out the following morning to set a record of his own in what would be his Ashes swansong, at least in Australia. He went past Geoff Boycott's 8,114 runs to become England's third most prolific run-getter, hitting fifteen boundaries in a knock of 71 off just eighty-six deliveries. But once again there was no wag in the tail and Crawley was left undefeated on 35 when we lost our last 5 wickets for only 30, setting the Aussies a target of 362.

At least we gave Australia something to think about and their captain Steve Waugh was probably pondering more than most because there had been talk that it could be his last Test. The series had not gone quite as well as he would have hoped from a personal point of view, but only those there could appreciate just how great the roar was when he walked out to bat. I had seen a lot of Steve Waugh on television and noticed how positive he always was, but so far this series he had not played in that manner. In the first three Tests he looked quite nervous and must have been feeling the pressure with a lot of people saying that he should not have been in the team.

Australia needed a captain's innings because their top order looked unusually vulnerable with Caddick generating a full head of steam to claim the wickets of Hayden, Ponting and Langer. Cometh the hour, cometh the man – Waugh must have written the script because as soon as he walked out there was a feeling that something special was about to happen. He scored the best hundred I have seen by an opposition player under that kind of pressure and spotlight. Waugh first of all steadied the listing ship in partnership with Martyn. The pair put on 90 for the fourth wicket, while Waugh needed just sixty-one balls to claim his half-century, becoming only the third player, behind Sunil Gavaskar and Allan Border, to score 10,000 Test runs.

Waugh simply went berserk with the bat and entered the last over of the day just a few short of his 100. He smashed a four off Richard Dawson from the last ball and the electricity generated by the loudest noise I have heard on a cricket field would have lit Sydney. The place erupted. Australian prime minister John Howard went into the dressing room to congratulate him. If that is the way he finishes, what a way to go, I felt at the time; but I had the suspicion he would want to keep playing Test cricket for a while yet, despite being stripped of the one-day captaincy.

The heroics would not be continued the following morning. Waugh went quickly for 102, but Adam Gilchrist came out and whacked a typical hundred. He is a player who always seems to come good when his side needs him most and they needed him then. We were not exactly ecstatic about his ton, but he is one of those players you do not mind watching bat because he is so exciting.

Australia held a one-run advantage after the first innings, but we were not too disappointed because we knew we would not be batting last on a wicket that would become uneven and take spin. First we had to bat well enough to set the game up and there I was walking out on a pair at the SCG, one of the world's most talked about grounds. Heading towards the middle with Trescothick, I said: 'Here we go, I'm on a pair again.' He replied: 'Don't worry. I'm at the other end backing up. You hit it and I'll run.' Sure enough, the third ball took an inside edge on to my pads, Trescothick called me and I was off the mark.

I was more relaxed now and flicked Gillespie into the stand for six. I really went after him; I knew that was the best ploy because of the nature of the wicket. They brought MacGill on and I was able to do the same to him. One boundary led to another with our supporters willing me and the team on to bigger and better things.

Trescothick's run of misfortune continued when he became Lee's hundredth Test victim by playing on, but Butcher and I added 87 for the next wicket and then Nasser and I added an unbroken 94 to take us to 218 for 2 in our second innings – a lead of 217. I had an unbeaten 113 to my name – I had been dropped on 102, ironically by Langer at mid-wicket. How he must have enjoyed that experience.

That third night in Sydney, Hoggard, Trescothick and I, with our girlfriends, booked a trip up Sydney Harbour Bridge. It takes three hours and at 10.30 p.m., after scoring a century and climbing all those stairs tagged to a wire, I was at the summit. There I was looking out over Sydney and for once I did feel like I was on top of the world. Matthew Hayden, I am sure, would not have shared my sentiments, although a couple of months later he would have to move over at the top of the world rankings.

It was quite a day and quite a way to warm down after a long knock. When you have been at the crease for a long time and do not finish until 6 or 6.30 p.m., you are still buzzing for the next three hours, living on adrenalin and taking in plenty of fluids because of dehydration. I tend not to eat much when I am batting, so after cereal and poached eggs for breakfast it is a fluid diet. I will eat a little during the day when fielding, but not when batting. I always find it difficult to sleep after a good knock because you replay everything in your mind. All the feelings and emotions, even the sounds in the ground, come back. When playing a day-nighter, especially if it is a tense finish after 10 p.m., I will not get a wink of sleep until at least 2 a.m. and often later, so that is why many players stay up and have a few drinks. There is not much of a physical problem, although the day after a long innings you feel stiff and tired, but those problems pass as soon as you start batting again.

We had 313 on the board the following day when Nasser Hussain left the middle with us having been 124 when he arrived. The momentum was certainly ours. Just when I was within distance of my first double hundred, a ball from Andy Bichel thudded into my pads and my six-and-a-half-hour stay at the crease was over, although replays suggested the ball would have comfortably cleared the stumps.

The way I played and the position we were in – we had entered the game staring at a whitewash – made it the best innings of my England career. It also emphasised the unpredictability of the world's greatest sport. Nobody ever knows what is around the corner. Steve Waugh gets a hundred one day and is out fifth ball the next. I got a century in Melbourne and then a duck the next knock. Now I had 183 very satisfying runs on the board and I had put the team in a position from where it would be possible to win. What is more, we had been put through a lot of pain during the two-and-a-half months we had been in Australia; the captain and coach had had a lot of media attention and the team had been taking a lot of stick both on the field and from the press. Oh how good it felt to have the Aussies on the back foot for a change. Nobody had got anywhere near them and now they were in danger of losing at home for the first time in four years. But the Aussies go out thinking of just one thing all the time – winning. They do not go out to lose. You have to beat them, and we were desperate to do it.

With a lead of 450, we knew much would depend on how Andy Caddick bowled. He had received some criticism through-out the tour, but had played well in Melbourne after returning from injury. With the unevenness of the pitch the taller bowlers would get most out of it and so it proved after we declared – yes, declared – leaving Australia needing 452 to win.

We could not have wished for a better start as the Aussies started their second innings knowing that, to win, they needed to break the record for the highest number of runs for a team batting last. If my lbw decision was debatable, the first Australian wicket to fall prompted loud shouts of 'No way' from the home dressing room when umpire Tiffin adjudged a ball from Caddick that crashed into Langer's pads had not pitched outside leg stump. Hayden followed shortly afterwards to the sound of breaking glass, of which more later, and then Ponting also discovered the folly of letting his legs do what his bat should have been doing. Three lbws, but we would take wickets any which way because at last we had the Aussies on the run. Just 25 for 3 from six overs was more than we could have hoped for.

Australia had not lost to England in Sydney in more than thirty years and entered the final day with 7 wickets remaining, needing to score another 363 for victory. I do not think it would have entered their minds that an option was to bat out ninety overs for a draw. It quickly became apparent that there was only going to be one result.

We knocked two or three of them over quickly, while they had Andy Bichel coming in six or seven stations ahead of his normal position, emphasising how important they thought the new ball would be and how quickly they wanted to knock the shine off it – Bichel does like to give the ball an almighty bash. But we had wickets in the bag from the previous evening and now Caddick ripped the heart out of them. The last rites were read to the Aussies just a few overs after lunch when their innings ended still 225 short of the target. Oh what joy, to be finally on the front foot against them and winning a Test match rather than suffering another drubbing. Being able to give our supporters something to shout about at last was another huge feeling of satisfaction and we did a lap of honour after the match to applaud and thank them. It was something we would have done in defeat, but to be able to do it in victory was special, very special.

Although the Ashes and series were long gone, an indication of the psyche of the Australian side was seen very clearly on the Sunday. Matthew Hayden, given out when he considered that the finger raised against him by the umpire should have been wagging in admonishment at the audacity of the English appeals, took a disliking to the glass-panelled dressing room door on returning to the pavilion. I viewed this as Hayden venting his frustration not just at being out but at not being able to register a series whitewash. There is no such thing as a dead rubber to an Australian and Hayden's Conan the Barbarian impersonation seemed to show that winning is the only thing.

Some of Hayden's subsequent comments confirmed my suspicions that Australia were also suffering from tiredness in Sydney, not least brought about by them spending two-and-a-half days in the field in Melbourne. Hayden admitted the team was jaded and there was an element of fatigue, since this was the side's eighth Test match in twelve weeks covering three different countries. It had been tough for the Aussies to main-

Australia v England (5th Test Match)

At Sydney Cricket Ground – 2, 3, 4, 5, 6 January 2003
Result: England won by 225 runs. Toss: England.

ENGLAND	First innings		Second innings	
M.E. Trescothick	c Gilchrist b Bichel	19	b Lee	22
M.P. Vaughan	c Gilchrist b Lee	0	lbw b Bichel	183
M.A. Butcher	b Lee	124	c Hayden b MacGill	34
*N. Hussain	c Gilchrist b Gillespie	75	c Gilchrist b Lee	72
R.W.T. Key	lbw b Waugh	3	c Hayden b Lee	14
J.P. Crawley	not out	35	lbw b Gillespie	8
+A.J. Stewart	b Bichel	71	not out	38
R.K.J. Dawson	c Gilchrist b Bichel	2	c & b Bichel	12
A.R. Caddick	b MacGill	7	c Langer b MacGill	8
M.J. Hoggard	st Gilchrist b MacGill	0	b MacGill	0
S.J. Harmison	run out (Langer/MacGill)	4	not out	20
Extras	(b 6, lb 3, nb 13)	22	(b 9, lb 20, w 2, nb 10)	41
TOTAL	(all out, 127 overs)	362	(9 wickets dec, 125.3 overs)	452

Fall of wickets – 1st inns: 1–4 (Vaughan), 2–32 (Trescothick), 3–198 (Hussain), 4–210 (Key),
5–240 (Butcher), 6–332 (Stewart), 7–337 (Dawson), 8–348 (Caddick), 9–350 (Hoggard),
10–362 (Harmison).
Fall of wickets – 2nd inns: 1–37 (Trescothick), 2–124 (Butcher), 3–313 (Hussain), 4–344 (Key),
5–345 (Vaughan), 6–356 (Crawley), 7–378 (Dawson), 8–407 (Caddick), 9–409 (Hoggard).

Australia bowling:
1st innings: Gillespie 27–10–62–1, Lee 31–9–97–2, Bichel 21–5–86–3, MacGill 44–8–106–2,
Waugh 4–3–2–1.
2nd innings: Gillespie 18.3–4–70–1, Lee 31.3–5–132–3, MacGill 41–8–120–3, Bichel
25.3–3–82–2, Martyn 3–1–14–0, Waugh 6–2–5–0.

AUSTRALIA	First innings		Second innings	
J.L. Langer	c Hoggard b Caddick	25	lbw b Caddick	3
M.L. Hayden	lbw b Caddick	15	lbw b Hoggard	2
R.T. Ponting	c Stewart b Caddick	7	(4) lbw b Caddick	11
D.R. Martyn	c Caddick b Harmison	26	(5) c Stewart b Dawson	21
*S.R. Waugh	c Butcher b Hoggard	102	(6) b Caddick	6
M.L. Love	c Trescothick b Harmison	0	(7) b Harmison	27
+A.C. Gilchrist	c Stewart b Harmison	133	(8) c Butcher b Caddick	37
A.J. Bichel	c Crawley b Hoggard	4	(3) lbw b Caddick	49
B. Lee	c Stewart b Hoggard	0	c Stewart b Caddick	46
J.N. Gillespie	not out	31	not out	3
S.C.G. MacGill	c Hussain b Hoggard	1	b Caddick	1
Extras	(b 2, lb 6, w 2, nb 9)	19	(b 6, lb 8, w 3, nb 3)	20
TOTAL	(all out, 80.3 overs)	363	(all out, 54 overs)	226

Fall of wickets – 1st inns: 1–36 (Hayden), 2–45 (Ponting), 3–56 (Langer), 4–146 (Martyn),
5–150 (Love), 6–241 (Waugh), 7–267 (Bichel), 8–267 (Lee), 9–349 (Gilchrist), 10–363
(MacGill).
Fall of wickets – 2nd inns: 1–5 (Langer), 2–5 (Hayden), 3–25 (Ponting), 4–93 (Bichel), 5–99
(Waugh), 6–109 (Martyn), 7–139 (Love), 8–181 (Gilchrist), 9–224 (Lee), 10–226 (MacGill).

England bowling:
1st innings: Hoggard 21.3–4–92–4, Caddick 23–3–121–3, Harmison 20–4–70–3, Dawson
16–0–72–0.
2nd innings: Hoggard 13–3–35–1, Caddick 22–5–94–7, Harmison 9–1–42–1, Dawson
10–2–41–1.

Umpires: D.L. Orchard (South Africa) and R.B. Tiffin (Zimbabwe).
TV Umpire: S.J.A. Taufel (Australia).
Match referee: Wasim Raja (Pakistan).
Man-of-the-match: M.P. Vaughan (England).

tain their normal intensity, but he did pay tribute to our performance without being the slightest bit patronising. 'They played well,' he said. Praise enough from an Aussie, who said that his expectations of us had been fulfilled in that once the pressure of trying to win the series had disappeared, we started to enjoy our cricket more.

'I hope that positive intent is something England take away from this series as it was evident when they batted second time around through Vaughan and Trescothick. Both are boundary hitters and they came out looking to dominate. That has to be the way to play against us,' he wrote in the *Daily Telegraph*. I could not have agreed more.

Hayden believed that an important key to Australia's success had been the fact that our opening partnership had failed to fire and that had allowed the hosts to dictate terms early in our innings, so more often than not we never had a platform on which to build a large first-innings score. Unfortunately, he had a point.

I had been given the man-of-the-match award and made a thank-you speech. On top of that, to be awarded man-of-the-series in a 4–1 losing side and to have scored 630 runs at an average of 63 was a great feeling with which to start 2003. It gave me hope that the New Year would be just as good as the old one.

Some judges said that the man-of-the-series should have gone to an Aussie and maybe it should, but I was not complaining. My acceptance speech included thanking our wonderful supporters – I will never forget their response as they chanted my name. I hope I gave them a little bit of pleasure and I am sure they were delighted that we had won a Test at the end of a tough old series. Credit where it is due, for I also complimented the Australians on being a superior team and dominating the series. I doubt that I will ever play against a better side, but there again you never know what fate has in store. I would like to think that one day I will play in a superior force.

The beers started flowing and we had quite a few of them in their dressing room as we sat round in a huddle for about three hours until it all became a bit of a blur. It was good fun and I chatted with Justin Langer for the first time since the 'not out' ruling in Adelaide. I respect him massively on the pitch because he is a fantastic player, a true, gritty performer. He plays it hard, as they all do, but they are all good fun off the pitch. Nobody had more fun than we did in Sydney and I had my trophies to prove it, including a stump signed by all our boys and Aussie PM John Howard.

What a welcome relief it was to have a smile on our faces – a blessed relief from the relative torture of defeat after defeat. Some Australians, and indeed some English observers, offered the absence of McGrath and Warne as a mitigating factor for their failure. True, any side would be less for the loss of two such icons, but we had almost half a team missing for the entire tour. Our moment of glory was well deserved in any circumstances.

I have always believed that the whole is of far greater importance than any one part of the England machine, but I was truly pleased to have made an impression on what was my debut Down Under. I was very interested to read that Steve Waugh said he believed I could achieve whatever I wanted to as long as I did not get carried away.

I can assure the Aussie skipper that there is no chance of me being sucked or suckered into a lifestyle that will have an adverse effect on my cricket. I do have other things in my life, but I believe that if my exploits do find their way on to the front pages of the tabloids it will be because of what I have done on the field rather than in a nightclub. Even if there was a chance – and there is not – of me getting carried away, those around me would soon be pulling on the reins to keep me in check.

I know just how unpredictable cricket is. Nothing should ever be taken for granted, and I may not have another year in the sun quite like the one I experienced in 2002. The runs I scored against Sri Lanka, India and Australia meant that when Matthew Hayden started having a comparatively lean time in the West Indies, I was promoted to the number one-ranked batsman in the world. But carried away? Never. I will admit that I have changed, but not in a way that has necessitated an increase in cap size. When I first came into the England team, I may have looked calm, but my insides were a tumble dryer. Now, although I am not without my own butterfly collection, especially when I am preparing to bat and until I have 20-odd on the board, I am far calmer than I have ever been.

As long as my body holds up, and for a twenty-eight-year-old I have had more than my fair share of breaks, tears, pulls and suspect knees, I hope to be around deep into the next decade. That means looking after myself and I have never been frightened of putting in the hours and keeping away from the bright lights. But change? Well maybe I will, but I hope only for the better.

A triangular one-day series with Australia and Sri Lanka followed the Tests. Having batted for quite some time in the two back-to-back Tests, my knee was causing some grief and it was decided I would be better having some rest and rehab. So, with the World Cup in mind, first I missed the two one-dayers, including the game against Australia in Hobart.

Pre-Christmas it had not been too bad for the one-day team because the World Cup squad had not been announced and there were players fighting for places. It became tougher after the holidays because the squad was named and did not include some of those currently involved in the Test series. It was very hard for the management and the players missing out to focus their minds. It is extremely difficult for everybody to be locked in on the same thought patterns when people are soon going in all directions. At the time, even those en route to South Africa did not know whether they were going direct or via home.

I had suspected for some time that there was little to separate the one-day teams of Australia and England, although the records tell a different story. Heaven knows when we last beat them, but I was convinced that an end to the run of Aussie dominance was not too far away. My convictions were unfounded.

Even with a 165-run opening stand from Trescothick and Nick Knight in Hobart, we still could not force a win in the qualifying games for the VB final as Australia confirmed their place. Seven wickets fell for just 99 runs in the final twenty overs and we fell 7 short of the target, leaving our own qualification to a later date. Our route to the best-of-three final would come via a bonus point gained in defeat, again by Australia, in Adelaide.

I returned for the third match, against Sri Lanka in Adelaide, one we had to win to stay in the tournament. It was great to be back playing limited-overs cricket because I do love the game. Unfortunately, due to injuries, I have missed quite a few. It was also good to be back in Adelaide where the ground is exceptional. I had scored a hundred there and what a feeling it was to be back in the dressing room, seeing my name up there with 177 against it. It is there forever and nobody will take it down. It is a truly wonderful feeling.

It is always difficult going from five-day to one-day cricket because there is a different atmosphere in the game, but it was good to feel I was still in form. More important, I was mentally sharp, and that for me is the key to batting. I was switched on and clued into the job. Unfortunately, we did not score as many as we would have liked. Nick Knight, who was in great form throughout the Test series, having arrived at the start of it in such poor form that he did not know how to spell the word bat, let alone which end to hold it, scored 40-odd and I got a quick 20-plus, but our score was within Sri Lanka's reach. We sneaked a win after Nasser ran out Jayasuriya on 99, while I was pleased to play my part with the ball, bowling seven of one end's last eight overs. It was a good win and gave us a chance of reaching the best-of-three final.

There had been mixed emotions before the game. We knew if we won we could go through to the final, but if we lost we were aware that we would be having two-and-a-half weeks at home before the World Cup. I reckon a few of us were thinking about the comfort of twenty days in our own beds, but it shows the character of the side that we wanted to get to the final.

The bookmakers had us as long-odds outsiders and their pessimism looked justified in the first match in Sydney. We made just 117 and Australia needed only seventy-four balls to reach their target – a remarkable run rate even by high one-day standards.

A lot had been made of reports that some of the squad had asked the ECB if it would be possible to nip home for six or seven days before the World Cup campaign started. Some in the media may have thought we were hoping to lose the first two of the best-of-three final so we would have time at home. There is no truth in that whatsoever. The lads just wanted a few days away from one another at home. When you have been in one another's pockets for four months, things do start to get on your nerves and bring out the aggression. That is not what you want leading into a World Cup.

It was made pretty clear to us that going home was not part of the agenda. We had several meetings about it, and asked if the ECB would pay the air fares but they would not. They would not stand in the way of anybody who wanted to go home at their own expense and so the decision was left to individuals. Steve Harmison was given special dispensation and allowed a week's leave because he had not seen his son born the previous November. A few players said they were prepared to fund their own trip back – an indication of just how much pressure we were under as a team. That players would dip into their own pockets for four nights of freedom at home proved just how ridiculous our winter schedule had been.

However, it was apparent that the Zimbabwe issue – whether or not England should go there – would soon have to be faced and it would have been difficult to get five days of peace and quiet at home with people knocking on the door all the time and phoning for our views. The collective decision was taken that it would be best if we stayed away and had three or four days break in Sun City rather than four or five days hassle at home.

So we had no reason at all not to give it our all in the second game of the final in Melbourne because we were staying away from home win or lose. We had to win to take the series into a decider and lost the toss on a boiling hot day. Australia elected to bat on what looked a grade A track. Freddie Flintoff made his comeback after several months spent recovering from injury and, with Caddick bowling brilliantly with the new ball, we looked a really good unit that day. We restricted them to 225 and maybe it should have been a few less, but Bradley Hogg played exceptionally well.

We lost 3 wickets early and then Nasser and I put on a few before the skipper went and Stewart and I added more. We had the game, to all intents and purposes, won. We were both out for 60, but Paul Collingwood, who had come into the one-day team and done exceptionally well, looked as if he was seeing us home. Australia had other ideas in the shape of Brett Lee.

We needed 20 in five overs, but as soon as Lee bowled Flintoff with a 94 mph inswinging yorker there was a sense that there might be another twist in the tale because all we had left was our tail. For Blackwell, Caddick and Anderson even to put a bat on these minimum 90 mph balls was going to be a tough ask. Full credit to Brett Lee – he bowled as well as I have ever seen from a star bowler at the death in a one-day game. His pace and swing made it virtually impossible to score off him and he won the game for his side.

We were short by just a handful of runs, but I believe we showed on that occasion that on any given day we could match Australia. That is why one-day cricket is so fascinating. Any one of the top six in world cricket can beat any of the other sides. One superb performance by one man with bat or ball and the game is won. In Test match cricket, it takes a team effort.

That was the end of the Aussie leg of the winter, apart from a let-your-hair-down party in Adelaide for a couple of days. After a long and largely unsuccessful trip, there was quite a lot of relief among the boys, knowing that we could wipe the slate clean in our own minds and get to the World Cup with new thoughts, anticipating new challenges. So far, not so good, but a new opportunity was waiting in South Africa.

CHAPTER 11
NOT CRICKET

When we left Australia for South Africa the party had been whittled down to just those involved in the World Cup campaign. That made it easier for all concerned – fifteen players and management – to focus fully. You know you will be playing together for the next four or five weeks and that brings a common bond and collective spirit.

As soon as we landed in Johannesburg we were on our way to Sun City which was probably as good an alternative to going home as could have been found. Returning to England would have been our first choice, but standing on the first tees of the Gary Player Country Club and Lost City courses was an acceptable substitute. It is an unbelievable place catering for all tastes and bank balances.

We played a Ryder Cup-style format that was meant to last three days, but one side, not mine, had an unbeatable lead after two days so the third was scrapped. Paul Collingwood and Nasser Hussain beat Ashley Giles and me convincingly in four-ball better-ball and the following day I was up against Freddie Flintoff in a singles. We had some distinguished company.

Ryder Cup hero Darren Clarke joined us along with Mark Bell, who is the South Africa representative for my business advisers, International Sports Management.

Mark and I took on Darren and Freddie. Darren insisted we play off the back tees, an experience in itself for mid-handicappers. I beat Freddie in our match and I would like to think it was through my pure brilliance, but I suspect it had as much to do with Freddie losing twenty-two balls. I play off a twelve handicap and was delighted to drop no more than four shots on the back nine, which enabled my team to come from two down at the turn to a three and two victory, although Darren Clarke was more than generous with his shot allocation.

Not so Paul Collingwood. I have no hesitation in calling him an outright bandit on the golf course. He has an official handi-cap of nine, but could play easily off three. It is an absolute joke and none of the lads has enjoyed handing over their money to him. There is also a lot of debate about Nasser's handicap and sometimes things can get a bit aggressive because we are all so competitive. Alec Stewart announced that he did not play golf and then went round the Gary Player course in twenty-two over par, beating a less-than-amused Andy Caddick in the process.

All the same, that break was exactly what we needed as we built up a good spirit away from bats and balls. We still trained to keep up our fitness levels, but really what we needed most was rest and relaxation. It was an excellent few days of team bonding as we looked in at the casino's blackjack tables and had fun on the water slides and jet skis before heading back to

Johannesburg and then on to Port Elizabeth for the start of our World Cup campaign.

The security we received in South Africa was consistent and bordering on the excessive. We had two guards throughout the tournament and were accompanied everywhere we went outside the team hotel. I do not know if they were anticipating problems or were just over-cautious, but our guards were never more than a few paces from our sides throughout. On one four-hour coach journey from East London to Port Elizabeth we were even shadowed by a police helicopter. Flintoff and White hitched a ride in it for part of the journey.

The warm-up games were very relaxed and low key. It was just a question of giving everybody a bat and a bowl and working out what was best for each individual.

But soon we would be concentrating on something far more sinister, an issue that had to be addressed and ultimately cost us the chance to advance to the Super Sixes. We had to decide what to do about our opening match in Zimbabwe.

When planning my column in the *Daily Mail* it became clear as early as November 2002 that I would have to start thinking what to say about going to Zimbabwe. We were due to meet them in the first leg of the World Cup. This was an unwelcome prospect for me. I am a cricketer first and foremost; I read the newspaper back to front, and not necessarily all the way to the front, either. Nasser Hussain raised the issue in Melbourne over Christmas and we had the first of a long series of meetings in which we were urged to get ourselves up to date on the facts and think what we each wanted to do. With the immediate problem of attempting to contain the Australians in the forefront of our minds, it was easy to push the Zimbabwe problem on to a back burner. But the news stories would not go away. President Mugabe's atrocities were happening. It was not a Stephen King film. And we were in a situation where the patron of Zimbabwe cricket had declared himself the 'sworn enemy' of England.

But still my mind was not made up because I am a cricketer and all I want to do is play. At the back of my mind, too, was the knowledge that four points were at stake in Harare and they were points I would expect us to get to give our World Cup campaign the perfect start. Four points there and maximum against Holland and Namibia would virtually assure us of a place in the Super Sixes.

The English Cricket Board's line was that the safety of the players was of paramount importance, but until it was shown that our safety was at risk, their stance was that we should travel to Zimbabwe and fulfil our opening fixture. A number of politicians thought we should not be going, but the government seemed curiously slow to take a stand. They finally said that they did not want us to go, but it was down to us. However, when asked if they would compensate the ECB for loss of revenue, they refused.

Our own meetings meanwhile were growing more intense because the situation was coming to a head. The Professional Cricketers Association, and the Team England lawyers Harbottle and Lewis, were invaluable in their support of the players throughout this entire and unsatisfactory affair. Over one dinner in East London after a warm up game the only issue we were talking about was Zimbabwe. We would normally be talking cricket, the Premiership, sex, drugs and rock-n-roll, but here we were discussing our roles as political pawns in a game of death not cricket. I was as confused as I have ever been and it was not a nice feeling. Certainly in South Africa I did not hear one person say: 'Go, it's only a game of cricket.' The trouble was that it was not a game of cricket any more.

Security was our primary concern. We were blandly assured it would be no problem. Could we believe this? At the same time we could not be impervious to the mounting stories of atrocities. We learnt of bodies of people who had been murdered being tossed into bunkers on a Bulawayo golf course. Could we possibly play a game of cricket where that kind of thing was going on? Then there was the question of shaking Mugabe's hand. He had made it clear that if we refused we were signalling our opposition to his regime and might face prison. Security would be no help to us then. Nasser, as captain, was in a terrible position. If there had been a picture of him shaking hands with Mugabe, think of the headlines. But if he didn't, the prospect was chilling.

Decision time was fast approaching as we flew from East London to Cape Town where a hundred bats for the World Cup were waiting to be signed. The ECB failed to impress on the ICC the concerns and positions the England team were being put in. Then something happened that shocked the players and gave rise to several contradictory statements from the ICC security personnel. Tim Lamb, chief executive of the English Cricket Board, received a letter, posted in England on 6 January 2003, from the self-styled Sons & Daughters of Zimbabwe. It said:

Hands across the ocean – thanking the Barmy Army for their support after the Fourth Test in Melbourne, December 2002.

A spectacular firework display over Sydney Harbour Bridge heralds the New Year, with the final Test imminent.

Mark Butcher raises his bat to acknowledge the applause as he reaches three figures in the Fifth Test.

England stalwart Alec Stewart leaves the field in Sydney after passing Geoff Boycott's Test run aggregate.

Waugh zone – Aussie skipper Steve Waugh launches into the ball and scores his 10,000th Test run during the final match of the series in Sydney.

Matthew Hoggard holds nothing back with this lbw appeal during the Fifth Test, and Matthew Hayden starts to walk.

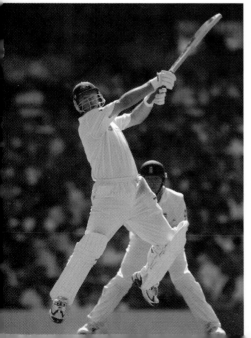

A rare picture of Aussie spinners Shane Warne (*left*) and Stuart MacGill together – all smiles despite the loss of the Fifth Test.

United in Victory – wicket keeper Stewart and I hold stumps while our team-mates celebrate success in Sydney with the flag of St George.

Nasser Hussain leads out England during the World Cup opening ceremony in Cape Town in February 2003.

The World Cup's exuberant opening ceremony is brought to a close.

Taking time out on South Africa's Port Elizabeth beach to reflect on a long winter away, March 2003.

At a press conference, the strain of the Zimbabwe problem shows on the faces of (*from left*) the PCA's Richard Bevan, Nasser Hussain and the ECB's David Morgan and Tim Lamb.

Coach Duncan Fletcher points England's players in the right direction during the build-up to the World Cup.

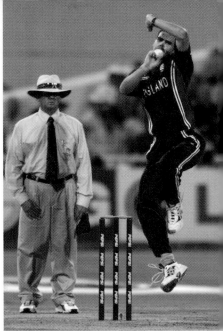

Namibia's Jan-Berry Burger goes on the offensive during England's second match of the World Cup.

James Anderson puts Pakistan to flight with a four-wicket haul at Cape Town's Newlands ground.

Flintoff celebrates dismissing India's Sachin Tendulkar during England's fourth World Cup match in Durban.

Arm's length – there is no stopping Ashish Nehra as he celebrates taking my wicket during India's win in Durban.

Trescothick leans back and powers another six against Australia at St George's Park in Port Elizabeth.

Australia's Andy Bichel takes off after England skipper Nasser Hussain is bowled in Port Elizabeth.

Aussie batting heroes Andy Bichel (*left*) and Michael Bevan walk off after steering their side to victory.

The newly appointed one-day captain joins England predecessors on the wall of honour at Lord's.

Dear Mr Lamb,

This letter is coming from Harare, Zimbabwe, but it is going to be posted in Britain. Congratulations on your decision to come and play cricket in Zimbabwe.

We were interested to be informed that a spokesman of the Department of Culture stated: 'We are pleased the ECB has made it clear players will not take part in Mugabe's propaganda'. What a cynical piece of crap! By coming to Zimbabwe in the first place, your Players ARE, wittingly or unwittingly, taking part in Mugabe's propaganda.

Our message to you is simple: COME TO ZIMBABWE AND YOU WILL GO BACK TO BRITAIN IN WOODEN COFFINS!

Mugabe's thugs and a huge opposing group are like two chemicals waiting for a catalyst to spark a violent reaction. Your visit to Zimbabwe will provide precisely that catalyst and there's going to be one mighty bang. The England Players and a load of Zimbabweans will die in the carnage.

Of course, Mugabe and his henchmen will ensure you that they will protect you, and if you seek and accept that assurance are you not, in actual fact, conniving with his murderous regime? And all for what? Money? One Black Zimbabwean's life is worth a damn sight more than £5M.

So, all you can think of is money when Black men, women and children are being tortured, murdered, beaten up and starved on a daily basis. Did you know that there is a facility at Goromonzi, a few miles outside Harare, which looks like a covered public swimming pool? The only difference is that the pool is covered with concentrated Sulphuric Acid. Anybody who opposes Mugabe ends up in there – dissolved and with no trace left behind. A bit like the Concentration Camps in Nazi Germany, or is your memory so short that you have already forgotten?

Anyway, we know your Team. Come to Harare and you will die. And how safe are your families back there in the UK? Even if you survive, there are foreign groups who are prepared to hunt you and your families down for as long as it takes, and they will do that in your own very country.

Our advice is this: DON'T COME TO ZIMBABWE OR YOUR PLAYERS WILL BE LIVING IN FEAR FOR THE REST OF THEIR LIVES.

Yours sincerely

Sons & Daughters of ZIMBABWE

The feeling that swept the room as we read the death threat was one of pure, unbelievable concern for our families back home – unadulterated, blood-chilling fear. We knew such a letter could be a malicious hoax, but how could we gamble with our families' lives? Malcolm Speed, chief executive of the ICC, came to see us totally underbriefed and failed to address any of the security issues that were raised. The ICC continued to send out the most unhelpful of mixed messages. One minute they were denying the Sons & Daughters of Zimbabwe existed, the next it was revealed that the letter was already subject to a confidentiality agreement, indeed an arrest had already been made in Zimbabwe relating to the Sons & Daughters. As for Ali Bacher, the World Cup organiser, we never had a sight of him. A senior South African policeman assured us he got ten letters like that a day. We responded that that was his job but we were cricketers and if we received one letter like that in our lifetime it was one too many.

That letter tipped the balance for us. Our feelings were unanimous in a private vote. We did not want to go to Zimbabwe.

At this cliff-hanging point in proceedings we had to break off to attend the World Cup opening ceremony in Cape Town on 8 February.

There is only one word to describe the World Cup's opening ceremony – spectacular. It was a particularly poignant occasion for us because after a week spent listening to bullshit and lies, fantasy and fabrication we needed something completely different to re-unite us to the common cause. That windy evening in Cape Town and a cast of thousands did exactly that.

Lining up outside waiting for our turn to walk into the stadium at Newlands gave us the chance to relax a little bit, forget about politics and remember exactly what the precise purpose of our being in South Africa was.

Our choir was led and conducted by Freddie Flintoff and Ronnie Irani, who treated us to a murdered version of 'Rivers of Babylon', a kind of team theme tune dating back to a tour to Pakistan. Queen's 'Bohemian Rhapsody' was similarly strangled and the boys were in good form and voice by the time it came to take our bow. We received an unbelievable response from the huge crowd. Only the home nation was granted a bigger ovation and the whole atmosphere and ceremony made the hairs on the back of my neck stand to attention.

At roughly the same moment, a lot of players started to realise exactly what we were losing by not going to Zimbabwe. Those four points could prove crucial but they were the least of the equation. This is what I was thinking. If I go there, play a game of cricket and people lose their lives because I have done so, how am I going to live with myself? There's more to life than cricket. I love the game and it is my profession, but I will never be one who is just cricket-orientated. Once the game is finished, I enjoy doing other things. In twenty-five years' time when I am playing golf or mowing the lawn or having a white wine or two I do not want to look back and think, I went to Zimbabwe and played cricket and cost thirty people their lives.

I resented the fact that the final decision had been left in our hands. It was not too bad for me because, although this was my first World Cup, I had been around the scene for a few years; not so twenty-year-old Jimmy Anderson. This was his first winter with us and he had to put up with all this political garbage at a time when all his thoughts and energies should have been geared towards cementing a place in the side. It says much for the lad's character just how well he dealt with everything and if a star appeared at the World Cup it was definitely shining above his head. I also felt for Nasser and Alec because this was probably going to be their last World Cup and the previous two had also been tarnished by controversy. This was going to be no different when all they wanted was for it to go smoothly and let the cricket do the talking. Unfortunately, it was never going to be like that.

So now it was decision time. The whole squad sat in a room and we were finalising our thoughts and opinions with Nasser when the door burst open and in walked the ECB lawyer announcing the need for an urgent meeting. But we had had enough meetings and Nasser butted in to say: 'No. We're still discussing your request for our views.' However, the lawyer would not be put off, and then ECB chairman David Morgan walked in with Tim Lamb, and announced that the ECB was pulling us out of Zimbabwe for safety reasons. The only factor for them was one of safety and security; they were not prepared to fulfil the fixture in Harare because they had not received the necessary unequivocal assurances regarding the safety and security of the team, officials and their families. The ECB's decision had not been taken for moral or political reasons.

Interpol had been involved; investigations had revealed the authenticity of the Sons & Daughters. Not only that, but the letter had not been a hoax and they were planning to take action. The whole room went deathly quiet. We had been told that the group did not exist, but now we had proof that they did and were planning a catastrophe. We felt anger, betrayal and disgust and among all the emotions were a few tears. Players began to think of the people back home. What we had been put through for the last forty-eight hours leading up to the decision is something I never want to experience again.

At least we now knew where we stood in relation to playing the game in Zimbabwe. But would the ICC agree to switch the game or split the points? My gut feeling was that as soon as we told them we were not travelling, the four points would go out of the window. The ICC's stance was that unless safety was a concern, points would be deducted and they had said our safety would not be compromised by us travelling to Zimbabwe. The activity of Interpol did not impress them in the slightest. The entire issue was now in the talons of the legal eagles.

On what would have been the day of the Zimbabwe match,

Thursday, 13 February, we instead spent part of it in a team meeting with our psychologist, Steve Bull. The team was also split into random two-man partnerships and I was paired with Craig White. We were asked to challenge and support one another throughout the remainder of our stay. It seemed a good way to keep everybody on their toes because it had been a long, hard winter. It would be nice to have somebody driving you all the time. Craig would keep reminding me that we did not have long left before going home and to keep pushing myself and working. I would say the same sort of thing to him.

Towards the end of the meeting I remember somebody mentioning the three lions and then Alec Stewart made a great speech. It was his fourth World Cup and he spoke for five minutes about what it meant to him to represent his country and how the two previous ones had been débâcles. He described how he felt and what sacrifices had to be made to do well. It was a very moving speech and he had everybody's attention from start to finish. It also produced the motto for the coat of arms we created for ourselves. 'Remember what Al said' would become the buzzwords whenever we went on the pitch or needed to be reminded about what we were doing in South Africa.

A couple of days later we learned that we had been docked the four points for failing to fulfil the fixture against Zimbabwe. We thought the decision was a joke after the evidence we had presented. Nasser got everybody together and told us it was time to draw the line on the matter. If we won four out of our other five matches we would still go through and be able to stick two fingers up to the ICC.

The first of those five would be against Holland. Thank heavens we were on our way into the tournament. It seemed like the World Cup had been happening around us forever and yet we had not struck a ball in anger. Now was our chance.

CHAPTER 12
BANANA SKINS

Although most of the England team's thoughts centred on our preparation for the biggest festival in cricket, I would be lying if I said I had given no thought to all the other teams in the competition, and not just those in our group.

Pakistan are the most talented team in the world outside Australia. They have everything as cricketers – their batsmen are all free-scoring with shots all around the wicket and they have an unbelievable seam attack in Wasim Akram, Waqar Younis and Shoaib Akhtar. Add to all those qualities the mystery spin of Saqlain and you have the perfect ingredients for a one-day team. Unfortunately, in their case, the right ingredients do not always make the perfect mix because they have everything a team wants except one thing – a common bond. Instead of pulling together they seem to end up tugging in opposite directions. Waqar is a good lad and it beats me how he failed to get them together as a unit because they just did not perform at all, particularly on the day we played them. You have no idea which Pakistan team is going to turn up – the unbeatable one or the one that beats itself. In South Africa, they never looked like, or performed like, the team they should have been.

The West Indies are similar in that they can beat the world one day and struggle to beat an egg the next. They are a team in transition and have yet to replace the Courtney Walsh–Curtly Ambrose axis to spearhead their bowling. Much would depend on captain Brian Lara, but it seemed that too much rested on his bat.

Those who betted against New Zealand reaching the Super Sixes had not accounted for the spirit in the team. The loss of points because they refused to travel to Kenya would be no burden.

The world knew of the strength of India before they arrived and their reputation was not damaged. How could it be with such strength in depth in the batting line-up, headed by the little master, Sachin Tendulkar. If Sachin is on fire, the wicket is scorched and you can be staring at big numbers when you go out to bat. He is a match for anyone in the world and in Virender Sehwag they seem to have another in the same mould. They have tantalising spin in Harbhajan Singh and are a very experienced side through playing a great deal of one-day cricket. Javagal Srinath is their Glenn McGrath because he is always there or thereabouts and moves the ball both ways. Ashish Nehra made the most of day-night conditions in Durban to undo us and is capable of good spells in any conditions because he puts the ball in the right areas.

We also knew of Sri Lanka's one-day personality and that they are a match for anybody on their day. They would prosper while I think everybody expected South Africa, at home, to be a force. I also think they expected to win it, but probably talked a bit too much about it. They had batting in depth, good bowling, they had it all apart from a mystery spinner, but they did not perform or become the team we and they thought they would be. Herschel Gibbs is a fantastic player and wonderful talent, and does not seem to have been affected by the betting scandal involving the late Hansie Cronje, of which he was a part. But on the bowling side they did not have the third seamer to back up Pollock or Ntini.

As we prepared for our first match, we were well aware of one thing. The team to beat was definitely Australia.

Our practice and energy levels throughout the week had been good and now we had the release of finally moving on to the field instead of into a meeting room, and getting away, too, from the Indian restaurant waiter, taxi driver and every Brit we bumped into who only wanted to know about Zimbabwe, Zimbabwe, Zimbabwe. It was giving our heads a serious amount of ache, so being back on the pitch was a great aspirin.

We felt that Holland gave us the opportunity of some easy points, but we still had to focus on doing what was necessary to win because it was an international match and therefore a potential banana skin. It was crucial to get a good start; although this was our first match, we had already lost four points. We needed to win and show that we were together as a team. We already knew that the Zimbabwe issue had made us much more tightly knit – all for one and one for all.

Compared with players from the subcontinent who seemed to have been born with their pads on and had played innumerable one-day series, we were relatively inexperienced. This was my first World Cup game and I had not many more than twenty one-day internationals behind me. I had been coming in at five or six, but now I would be at the crease at the fall of the first wicket. It would have been preferable to me to go in first as I do in the Test matches, but Nick Knight had done extremely well in partnership with Marcus Trescothick and the decision to split them up would have been a difficult one. The next best thing was for me to go in at number three. I was grateful because Nasser could easily have come in first wicket down, but the current order gave us three opening bats – useful in the event of an early wicket.

There was a different feeling in the camp as we had breakfast. As Nasser said, it was nice to wake up on a Sunday morning feeling nervous and thinking about a game of cricket rather than another net or the inside of a meeting room. We were getting our blues on at last and starting our campaign. I had endured two of the longest weeks of my life and was thanking heaven that the waiting was over. We were now about to get on with what we were there for.

There was an hour and forty minutes before the match started, time for a quick check of the papers and television and a chat with our scorer and computer controller, Malcolm Ashton. We won the toss and elected to field, although many people outside the camp wondered why we had not batted and put on a big score, but our thinking was that it was better to put them in, restrict them to a low score and then knock them off quickly. We were showing our ruthless streak.

Nobody showed it more than Jimmy Anderson, who settled into the team more quickly than anybody I have ever known.

A year ago he was playing for Burnley and now here he was at a World Cup being thrown the new ball. He has a big match temperament and although he had not played ten games it seemed like he had been around for a long time. He was a breath of fresh air and he blew away Holland with four quick wickets to become man of the match and receive a gold watch.

His 4 for 25 in ten overs included almost half those runs coming in one over alone. Limiting the opposition with the new ball is always an important factor and occasionally a crucial one, and in Anderson and Caddick we had a pair who could not only trouble the best, but also tie them down. It was a slow, low pitch and although the Dutch showed some late aggression, primarily from Tim de Leeds, they were never going to amass enough runs to cause too many jitters. We needed just 142 to win.

After Trescothick went early, I joined Nick Knight and we had a few problems running between the wickets because it was so windy we could not hear one another's calls. I felt in good touch, even though it is not easy getting into a rhythm against slower bowlers when you are used to 90 mph deliveries. Still, despite a few scares that are all part and parcel of batting, it was nice to contribute with a 50 and head back to the hotel with a feeling of mission accomplished.

There is just no pleasing some people and the press did not cover our victory with any great enthusiasm. Nasser countered their lukewarm response by saying that success in 23.2 overs was comprehensive, no matter who the opposition was.

The pens would be similarly poised in attack mode should we falter against Namibia in Port Elizabeth. They are always tough games when you are expected not only to win, but to do so with a minimum of discomfort. Everybody's expectation levels burst the rafters and more often than not teams find themselves 40 for 3 or 4. Although not quite as bad as that, we were no different, everybody getting in and just as quickly out. After they offered us first use of a wicket that had some damp in it, we hooked, pulled and drove our way to a respectable 272, thanks mainly to the efforts of Marcus Trescothick, Alec Stewart and Paul Collingwood, who looks like he is going to take some shifting from the side. My own contribution was regrettably low – two boundaries through extra cover and backward square followed by a pull into mid-wicket's hands.

Everybody seemed to be chipping in, but nobody got a really big score and our return, considering the pitch and the strength of the opposition bowling attack, was somewhat lower than we should have been able to amass. More than 300 was not too much to ask, but it was more than we were able to deliver. Full credit though to Namibia coach Dougie Brown, the Warwickshire player, who had obviously done his homework and a lot of work with his players. They had a plan and, for more than a little of a long afternoon, it looked like it might be paying off.

Our hopes that this might be another comfortable stroll were reinforced in only the fourth over when Stephan Swanepoel did not get over a full-length delivery from Jimmy Anderson and allowed me to take a relatively easy catch at wide mid-on. But Jan-Berry Burger took a liking to our bowling and played a truly superb innings, putting Namibia in a position where they could contemplate victory rather than just respectability. He not only smashed us to all parts of the ground, but also did it with authentic cricket shots and not just slogs. They surprised us to the point that for a few overs we were made to think that our own worst nightmare was about to be realised. With twenty-five overs remaining they were looking at no more than 6 an over, eminently attainable, and I thought to myself that this was one embarrassment I would rather not be on the end of. Burger made 85 at a run a ball and a third-wicket partnership with Keulder ended just 3 runs short of a hundred. We did not bowl as cleverly as we would have liked on a slow wicket, but full credit to them for playing very well indeed.

Salvation was at hand, however, and a quick clatter of wickets allowed us to celebrate a 55-run win, a comfortable margin on paper, but one that had been anything but at one stage. There could be no self-congratulation because we all knew that the margin of victory should have been far greater. At least with eight points out of two games we could look forward to facing Pakistan, but only if we upped our game by 25–30 per cent. Anything less and we would be staring at defeat.

CHAPTER 13

OVER AND OUT

My manager, Andrew 'Chubby' Chandler, a larger than life character in every possible way, and his ISM company's cricket director, Neil Fairbrother, the former Lancashire middle-order bat who was one of the best England one-day players of his day, arrived in Cape Town from their Cheshire base as we travelled back there from Port Elizabeth. It is always nice to see fresh faces when you have been joined at the hip to the same people for such a long time and their arrival made for welcome relief, as well as a couple of entertaining dinners, particularly one in nearby Camp's Bay, arguably one of the finest places on the planet and I am not being paid to say that. Many of the lads were knackered and the chance to chill out for a couple of days was a pleasant diversion, so I spent one of the afternoons on the beach in the convivial company of Paul Collingwood.

The mood in the camp was noticeably upbeat as the match against Pakistan at Newlands grew nearer. There were some seriously good vibrations infiltrating the camp for a match that would mark the long awaited return of Ashley Giles to the team for the first time since breaking his wrist in Australia. Having come into the England scene at the same time and having been on every tour together, we tend to do most things in one another's company, and Ash has been a mate of mine for some time now.

The atmosphere in Cape Town throughout the build up had to be experienced to be believed. We knew we would have plenty of support, but not the levels it would reach. When we arrived, the flags of St George were flying from just about every hotel balcony window and the beaches were packed with Brits. Even when we practised on the Thursday and Friday before the day-nighter, our followers were out in force, and then when we arrived at the stadium, overlooked by the awesome Table Mountain and the less than awesome Castle Brewery, we got an idea of what it must have been like for FA Cup final teams driving along Wembley Way. There were flags and replica shirts everywhere and the whole feeling gave the boys an enormous lift going into the ground.

Of the 28,000 in Newlands, at least 26,000 must have been from Britain and I even heard of one man and his son from Leeds who had flown out for the weekend to take in just this match. They, like all the other supporters and the team itself, were well aware of the importance of the toss in Cape Town and there was an almighty roar when we won it and elected to bat. The wicket looked good, the conditions would be in our favour and there was a growing feeling of confidence without complacency. We knew we had to play as close to our best as possible because Pakistan represented a formidable force, worthy of the utmost respect, and capable of beating anybody, should the mood take them.

We did not make the most auspicious of starts. Trescothick had not been enjoying the best of luck and his run continued when Wasim Akram, the pick of the Pakistani bowlers, found the outside edge with an inswinger and the agile Rashid Latif collected another victim for the pair of them. I went in to witness Shoaib Akhtar in the distance close to the boundary edge. He was at the end of his run-up, generating speeds previously unknown at World Cup level. You could sense the electricity in the crowd as the speed gun registered closer and closer to 100 mph and his world record.

With Shoaib running in like that and the crowd buzzing as Pakistan looked like getting on top, I knew it was important to switch the emphasis on to them. Attack would be the best form of defence against such hostility. Shoaib eventually got to the 100 mph mark, becoming the only player to have sent such an express delivery down twice, and the ground erupted. But I sensed he was not in the mood for celebrating because by this time we were beginning to cart him all over the pitch, and when he went for 24 in two overs it was too many for skipper Waqar Younis, who brought himself on at first change.

I had already had one scare when the first ball I received hit the top edge and ballooned up for a simple catch, but as soon as I hit it, the umpire's hand was out for no-ball and I knew the Pakistani celebrations were in vain. We advanced quickly until Waqar joined the attack and Nick Knight went after him, but to no avail. Nick was undone by the bounce, charging down the wicket, and Razzaq caught him at mid-off. Nasser also attacked, but went caught behind chasing an away swinger.

The run rate increased, unsurprisingly, with Alec Stewart's

arrival at the crease and we shared a run-a-ball 50 before Shoaib returned and I cracked him straight to gully while Stewart fell to Afridi. It was then that Paul Collingwood emphasised just how important he is to the team by slowing the Pakistan advance through the middle order. He held his end up and the team together. Collingwood just played clever cricket, picking up the ones and twos, aided and abetted by Freddie Flintoff. We finished with 246, a score I always felt we could defend. I did not envy them their task as the sun fell, the dew formed and Jimmy Anderson came racing in.

There is only one way to describe the way the youngster bowled – sensational. He got the ball to both swing and zip and, although the conditions were favouring the bowler, he still had to put it in the right places. He did it, ably backed by Caddick, Flintoff and White, with stunning regularity and Pakistan succumbed, although not even we thought that they would fall more than 100 runs short with nineteen overs unused. Indeed the margin of victory would have been even greater but for a late blast from Shoaib, who gave the Pakistan supporters something to cheer about at last with 43 off just sixteen deliveries, including five fours and three enormous sixes. Even the England supporters enjoyed it because by this time they knew the match was in the bag.

A case could have been made for Paul Collingwood to get the man-of-the-match award because he came to the helm and steadied the ship when wave after wave of Pakistan aggression was sweeping over us, but Jimmy Anderson deserved it not just for the quality of the batsmen he got out – Inzamam, Youhana, Anwar and Latif – but for the deliveries he got them with.

Jimmy's father and grandfather sitting in the stand must have been the proudest people in Newlands as the opening bowler zipped through ten overs on the bounce. I doubt that Nasser was even tempted to give him a rest because he looked like taking a wicket with every ball. The captain knew the importance of nailing Pakistan to the ground because even with six down they still had some handy performers to come. Jimmy's four-for was a superb spell and he really did look the part. To have won a match for England in what was the biggest day of his sporting life and at such a young age will live with him until his grandchildren get fed up with hearing about it.

My participation in our fielding was restricted to that of spectator because I had a problem with a calf muscle. A couple of years earlier I had a similar problem and was out for two months so I was not going to risk another lengthy absence. I had twisted it practising and then it tightened up while I was batting. Since I was not going to bowl in the match, it seemed sensible not to risk it so that I would be fit for the next one.

At least I took part in the on-pitch celebration afterwards as we walked the ground to applaud our magnificent supporters. They really are the best in the world – Barmy, unbelievable and totally supportive. They could not show us enough how they appreciated our efforts and even gathered close to the dressing room after the match was over. It is always great to rejoice at a win, but even as some of our players joined the supporters in singing and chanting, I could not help thinking to myself that maybe we were peaking with our euphoria too soon. I did not want us to think that we had qualified already because we still had two massive matches to come and we had to win one of them against India or Australia. The mental aspect is huge in cricket and the last thing I wanted was for the side to believe that beating Pakistan at Newlands would be enough for us to go through.

We chilled out by the pool at our hotel afterwards, enjoying one another's company as well as that of Phil Tufnell. The Cat is always on good form and hugely entertaining and this was the first time we had bumped into him at the World Cup, where he was working for BBC Radio. He was already bordering on the worse for wear when he joined us and pretty soon he was in good company.

All heads were clear by the time we arrived in Durban, although judging by the number of Indians there when we arrived it was more like coming into Bombay. The gap between matches had enabled me to rest my calf and a scan showed there was no tear so I should be all right to face Sachin and co. Rumours of storms brewing were proved inaccurate as the wind changed direction the night before the game, so we knew our fate was in our own hands and not those of Michael Fish.

We were far more relaxed about the toss than we had been in Cape Town because we had heard that even in day-night matches, the side batting first did not necessarily hold a huge advantage. Statistics showed that sides batting second had won an equal number of matches. How wrong we were. Unfortunately, the norm was not the rule here in Durban because only later did we discover just how important it had been to call correctly. The pitch would do more, much more, as the day progressed. It was a costly discovery.

Our bowling and fielding could not be criticised and Freddie turned in a magnificent spell of 2 for 15 in ten successive overs. We were relatively happy to have restricted them to 250, but we quickly got a rude awakening when it came to our turn to strap on the pads.

Nick Knight, who had not quite hit the heights in South Africa that he reached in the VB Series against Sri Lanka and Australia, was run out by a Jonty Rhodes-style pick up and throw from Mohammed Kaif in only the second over. It was not the bowling that surprised me when I got to the wicket, but the light. I could not believe how dark it was. The lights were not as they had been in Cape Town – and ours were going out.

It was just like batting indoors where the ball skids on and you do not have time to play your shots. Zaheer Kahn was gathering pace off the pitch and with the light as bad as it was, we could not have asked for worse conditions in which to try to reach our target. I knew we would have to play out of our skins to get anywhere near and it proved a task too far. We fell woefully short.

Ashish Nehra bowled a magnificent spell to take 6 for 23, which at that stage represented the third best figures in World Cup history. Still, it was very disappointing to lose in the manner we did, particularly after playing so well against Pakistan. But we had to be realistic. We had had the luck and the best of the conditions in Cape Town and now it had evened itself out in Durban.

At least there were positives, not least the contribution of Flintoff, who followed his great spell with the ball to hit 63 off seventy-four balls. This is the standard we should expect from him now on a regular basis because he is without doubt one of the world's most talented cricketers and capable of heroic deeds on a more consistent basis.

Freddie's performance was deserving of a better outcome than an 82-run defeat, but I do not think that any player ever feels that he has been let down by the others, no matter how he has played. When I was getting my hundreds in the Ashes series and we were still losing, I never once thought, you bastards have let me down. I know there will be days when I get a duck and somebody else gets a hundred and we still lose. It is something every player has to accept.

Our luck had evened out and it added something to the debate about whether, in such a big event, winning the toss should have such a big bearing on the outcome of matches when played day and night. I do not feel it should and for the future I feel they should stick to day games only. I know it is quite a spectacle under lights, but it should not mean that a match could almost be determined by the toss of a coin. In South Africa and England, day-night matches can become something of a lottery, although in Australia and on the subcontinent they are not affected anywhere near as much.

India did ask for their semi-final to be changed to a day game and, although I understand that players cannot be seen to be ruling the game, I do not think switching just one game would have affected the entire World Cup. Their request was rejected, but surely it is better if everybody is on a level playing field, particularly in places where conditions do vary so considerably depending on the time of day.

Beaten, but not dispirited, we made our way to Port Elizabeth again in preparation for the decisive group game against Australia, victors in our previous thirteen one-day internationals.

With several days to go before the showdown, we relaxed on the golf course, although being thumped by Nasser and Collingwood is not my idea of relaxation. When we got down to the serious business of preparing for the match everybody was in top gear. We knew the importance of the game and to a man we felt that if anybody could beat Australia we were that team. We also knew we had to because our chances of progressing to the Super Sixes if we did not were minimal at best.

Here we were, back at St George's Park, and the things that stood out most were the flags of St George. There were hundreds of them as our followers turned up in their thousands again, praying that we could finally put one over the Aussies. Clashes between us have rarely been closer, although the decider in the VB series had been one of those where it was impossible to determine the outcome until it actually happened. This match would be exactly the same and, unfortunately, the result would follow the same pattern.

We could not have started much better because Trescothick, out of sorts for most of the winter, finally got on top of Glenn McGrath and the scoreboard ticked over merrily. The great man did not find his line and length and both Trescothick and Nick Knight went for him. We were only in the eighth over when the 50 came up and the Aussies were not a set of happy bunnies. If we could see off their spearhead with the ease that we did, then the wicket suggested there might be runs aplenty against change bowlers. It is typical of Australia that when one component of the engine splutters another fires on all cylinders. Step forward Andy Bichel. Suddenly from 70/0 we were 87/5 in their eighteenth over and staring down Bichel's barrel.

Bichel's fifth ball tempted Knight into steering a catch to slip and two balls later I got the faintest of nicks and Adam Gilchrist did the rest behind the stumps. Nasser was clean bowled and then McGrath found the outside edge and Trescothick was on his way back after looking as if he was going to produce the kind of one-day knock he had done so often in the past.

Stewart and Collingwood tried to stem the flow of wickets and did so for a few overs, but when the latter tried to chop Bichel he succeeded only in edging to Gilchrist and we had lost 5 wickets in next to no time. It was then that Stewart ground out a score and Flintoff showed just how responsible he could be as a batsman when the situation demanded it. This maturity can only be of great importance and encouragement to England for years to come. They added 90 for the sixth wicket and although it took twenty-five overs, it was more than we could have hoped for little more than an hour earlier.

Bichel finished with 7/20 and we totalled 204/8 in our fifty overs. It did not seem either many or enough to most judges, but I felt it was a decent score on a slow and crumbling wicket. The ball was stopping, so scoring was not as easy as some thought. If Australia came out and went at it as they normally did, we would have a chance because it was not the kind of track that you could be too free-spirited on. And so it proved, as Andy Caddick threatened to do for us what Bichel had done for the men in gold and green.

Caddick was on fire as he tempted Matthew Hayden into pulling one to Ashley Giles at mid-on and then I managed to juggle but hold on to a top edge from Gilchrist down at third man. Martyn went lbw and we were into them. Aussie skipper Ricky Ponting gave a reminder that it is not the most astute thing to drop one short just outside the off stump when he is at the crease when he pulled Caddick for a mighty six, but three balls later he tried the exact same shot and Ashley Giles held on to a fine catch at long leg.

We had them at 96 for 4 and were beginning to fancy our chances when Craig White managed to break up a partnership of 63 in twenty overs between Darren Lehmann and Michael Bevan by having the former caught behind. Giles chipped in with a couple and when White ran out Brett Lee with a magnificent throw, it looked like we would finally end our run against Australia and qualify for the Super Sixes. We thought victory was ours. We thought wrong.

Against Australia there always seems to be a spoiling factor that cannot be accounted for and Bevan, not for the first time, assumed the role of national hero. Bichel, if he had not already done enough with the ball, was his chief ally. Gradually, from a position of 8 down and 90 needed, they nudged Australia closer to the target. I remained convinced that somewhere along the line they would offer a chance, but not one came our way. It was amazing, one of the greatest escape acts of all time.

Nasser came in for some stick for giving Jimmy Anderson the penultimate over instead of Caddick, but that was hindsight criticism because the youngster had bowled such a good one immediately before. Unfortunately, I ended the winter as I started it – letting a soft one through my legs. But by then Bevan had proved what a great one-day batsman he is.

We had come so close to beating them now on three or four occasions out of the last five and still had not managed it, but I left the game feeling that our day may not be too far away against this lot. They were hammering everybody else so we cannot have been that bad because we were the only team who came anywhere near to giving them a game. But for us the game was up, barring miracles elsewhere.

We really should have won the match and had we done so we would only have had to beat Kenya to go through to the semi-finals and once you are there anything can happen. We were a smidgeon away and I believe we came that close to doing very, very well.

Mathematically, it still was not all over, but it was out of our hands and we had golf clubs in them when we heard that the match between Zimbabwe and Pakistan had been washed out so we were out. An hour later Nasser Hussain was sitting at a press conference announcing to the world that he was quitting as one-day captain. It was an interesting decision and one that interested me as much as, if not more than, anybody else, not that I realised at the time that I would soon be appointed his successor.

CHAPTER 14

HOME TIME

We were devastated to be knocked out of the World Cup, and left brooding on what might have been, but at least there was the blessed relief of going home. Not so Australia. They remained to fight another day, and another, and another.

The only way I thought Australia might lose, once into the Super Sixes stage, was on the wicket at Port Elizabeth, which would take spin, when they faced the Sri Lankans. If Murali was on top form and did something special, there was the chance of an upset.

There was a stage in the match when Australia were in a bit of trouble, but Andrew Symonds got them out of it, not for the first time in the tournament, with an unbeaten 91 backed by some fine support from Andy Bichel again. Once they had a score of 212 on the board on that track and with their attack, there was only ever going to be one result, unless something extraordinary happened.

If the Sri Lankans had won the toss and batted and put on a score of 200 plus, they would have had the Aussies under some real pressure and maybe that was the one stage of the tournament where Ponting's power players could have been vulnerable. But when the match went to a Duckworth Lewis decision because of rain, Sri Lanka were way behind target at 123 for 7.

Australia and India remained to complete the formalities and nobody was surprised when the World Cup final turned into such a one-sided game.

The Aussies are that good. They can handle any pressure and situation and they are the best team in the world by a margin, and it is quite a big one. It is up to the rest of us to bridge that gap because the way the Australian production line keeps on churning out world-class players makes me think their standards are only going to improve. The rest of the cricket world must move to keep pace, and fast.

From the moment Adam Gilchrist and Matthew Hayden set about the Indian attack with a savagery rarely seen outside an abattoir, there was never going to be any other result on the Wanderers pitch in Johannesburg. It might not have been made in Australia, but it was certainly made for Australia and how they exploited it.

Australia may have been without Steve Waugh, Shane Warne and Jason Gillespie, but it mattered little. They were defending a 100 per cent record throughout the World Cup and the Indians were powerless to prevent them as Ponting, Waugh's successor as captain, played an innings of stunning strokeplay and power. His 140 was a lesson in the good, the better and the incredible, while his 234-run partnership with Damien Martyn – clubbed in just one ball more than thirty overs – allowed Australia to set a record target of 360 for the Indians to chase. Once Glenn McGrath – as he so often does –

accounted for the opponent's most lethal weapon, Sachin Tendulkar, in the first over, the game was over.

Hayden had not had a big World Cup and I thought the stage was set for him, but he got to 30 and then got out. Ricky Ponting is just a fantastic player and he is one of the few that I would pay to watch bat. He's got all the shots, all the way round the wicket and he does not really block many. If it is short and fast he just keeps taking the bowlers on and I can pay him no greater compliment than to say that he is a guy a lot of players from around the world will have looked at and decided to try to emulate. It does not matter what hemisphere or time zone, he always seems to have the shots for the occasion and the pitch.

The Wanderers was ideal for him because it bounced a bit and any wicket that does that for Ponting is one that he has rolled up under his arm and laid out in the middle for himself. He is so strong off the back foot and cuts and pulls and hooks probably as well as anyone in world cricket. Anything short is going to find a boundary somewhere and anything up to him he drives well. When his feet are going as he likes he is one of the best players in the world for his team and for the rest of us to watch because he scores at such a vast rate of knots. He is always giving his bowlers plenty of chance to get the opposition out.

I was not at all surprised that he succeeded Steve Waugh as one-day captain and am equally sure he will do the same eventually in the Test team. Although Warne was mentioned, Ponting has always been the one who seemed to be born to be leader, not least because of an astute cricket brain that has developed through playing a lot of cricket from a very early age. He bats in the same position in the one-day and Test teams and his records are impressive.

Australia has such a talented lot of players – McGrath, Lehmann, Hogg, Symonds, Gilchrist, Bichel and I might as well include all the rest, because all the one-dayers and indeed the Test team seem to have a bit of an input. When you play against them they have eleven captains on the pitch and that aspect has made a big contribution to their success over the years. Any coach will tell you that a team of eleven captains is the ideal. You do not want just one guy out there telling everybody what to do, pulling all the strings and shouting all the time. You want eleven people advising and really thinking about the game. With the Aussies, every single one always seems to be thinking about every situation.

So what can we learn from them? As a nation, they have a great structure right back down to kids' level. Their government puts a big emphasis on sport, not just sport as a collection of games and activities, but succeeding in sport. It is not just the taking part but the winning that they focus on. All the schools seem to set aside Wednesday as a day when they play sport all day, and what great facilities they have to play in. The government backs their schools with money to ensure they always have the best. All right, they have a fantastic climate all the year round, but most of the schools seem to have a swimming pool and a love for sport.

There are so many jobs created by sport – it is not just the eleven on the pitch, but the marketing, management, grounds-men and so forth. I am convinced that we should put a lot more emphasis on sport, not just for the playing side but also in the area of management, marketing and accountancy. Maybe there should be a subject on the school curriculum embracing all aspects of sport, and we should be teaching it from the age of eleven. That seems to be how Australia have their education geared.

For example, there is a school at the WACCA where Freddie and I were in the swimming pool one day doing a few lengths with the kids. We were swimming along and one of them looked at me and said in typical Aussie fashion: 'Why aren't you training?' I replied: 'Never mind me training, why aren't you doing lessons?' He just said: 'This is my lesson.' I asked him what he meant and he said: 'We have swimming lessons three times a week and then we go in the classroom and talk about it.' They cater for everything. There were sixteen school outdoor nets, three separate ovals for playing cricket, five soccer pitches, rugby pitches. Name the sport, they had the facilities for it.

It was not a public school, just a regular establishment catering for all age groups and standards. They all seem to be like that, so maybe it is not surprising that they have a conveyor belt of talent churning out future champions. The kids must love growing up in Australia and I certainly would not have minded having similar facilities and the opportunity they allow when I was at school. Their academies develop potential, but we have little if anything to compare. How many schools in Britain have swimming pools? About 80 per cent in Australia have them, so no wonder they produce good swimmers. The only surprise is that they are not born with webbed feet.

It is also important to have a national team to look up to

because kids only follow success. Now all of them want to be cricketers or rugby players, swimmers or athletes. You name it, Australians seem to be world class at it, and even their soccer team looks pretty good. It is a different culture. Whatever we enter – cricket, football, rugby – we always think we can win. We went to Australia to win the Ashes and everybody thought we could do it. Realistically, we were miles behind them. We would have had to play at 120 per cent and they would have had to have five injuries for us to manage it. It was optimistic for us to go there thinking we could do it, but it is an English mentality to think that whatever competition we enter – Wimbledon with Tim Henman, the World Cup with David Beckham – yes, we can win it. It is amazing. Unfortunately, we are a bit behind in just about everything, although our rugby union players might disagree, and it all goes back to the structure of sport. The Aussies have it right.

You only have to watch them and see the infectious enthusiasm they have and the way they all enjoy it, but I think, as a nation, the thing we can learn most from them is just how big an emphasis they place on sport and the importance of it. The money they plough in must be huge, and the coaching they have is of the highest quality.

You can learn from them. When their coaches and cricketers come to Britain, you do collect valuable knowledge – Darren Lehmann at Yorkshire is a case in point – but you do have to go a lot further back to see where we could learn most. They have a pyramid in place with the international team at the pinnacle of it.

Having said that, my personal World Cup team would not

include all eleven Australians because there are players from other parts of the globe who would force their way into the side. I have deliberately omitted any of my English colleagues, although I can think of at least one I would like to include. I will leave it to them and you to guess who it might be and in whose place he would have been selected.

Here is my own World Cup team: Tendulkar, Gilchrist, Ponting, Lehmann, Bevan, Cairns, Klusener, Bichel, Lee, McGrath, Murali. Twelfth man: Gibbs.

CHAPTER 15
FORWARD THINKING

There had been a suspicion throughout the winter in the England dressing room, and a few rumours outside it, that Nasser's tenure of the one-day captaincy would end as soon as our World Cup fate was determined. In fact, Nasser himself had hinted that he would be calling it a day and, sure enough, as soon as the weather put paid to the last, lingering hopes we had of staying in South Africa, the skipper stood down. The newspapers went into overdrive about establishing the identity of his successor. I wanted it to be me.

In the circumstances, I had, of course, considered the possibility of being offered the captaincy, but it was not something that kept me awake at night. I went about my business, playing the way I like to play, and never pushed it. It's not my style to shout along the lines of 'I must be the next captain or I'm taking my bat home'. I was happy to leave events in the hands of fate because I believe things come to those who deserve and warrant them.

My name was bracketed along with the media's other front runners – my opening partner Marcus Trescothick and Surrey skipper Adam Hollioake, another good friend who had enjoyed much success in the one-day arena. Marcus had been vice-captain and he openly admitted he wanted to step up, but as soon as I got it he rang and said, 'Good luck. I'm right behind you,' and he didn't mean with a knife in his hand. Ask everybody who has captained him and I'm sure they will all say that you could not wish for a better person alongside you. You know what you are getting – a world-class player and team man. You can't ask for more than that.

Adam had made it clear in the media that he thought I should get the job. 'For the future of English cricket,' he'd said, 'Vaughan should be the man in charge, not me.'

I was called by the chairman of selectors, David Graveney, and the coach, Duncan Fletcher, and asked my opinion on different issues, which I gave. I explained how I would do the job and the reasons why I thought I was the man to take it on. Then I simply said to them, 'You've seen how I operate, so it's up to the selectors and hierarchy to decide if I'm the man.'

They offered me the job some days later, just ten minutes before I was due to tee off at the Hillside Golf Club, next door to Royal Birkdale on the Lancashire coast. I was given twenty-four hours to mull it over before someone from the ECB would ring to ensure that I still wanted the job and would accept it. That was a day I will never forget. European Tour winner Mark Foster was my playing partner and we were up against my manager, Chubby Chandler, and his lawyer, Dougie Heather, in a group of guys that included Aston Villa manager David O'Leary and ISM's cricket director Neil Fairbrother. Fossy and I, far more Fossy than me, hammered Chubby and Dougie and then we all went off to watch Manchester United in the Champions League at

Old Trafford. I spoke to a number of people – friends, family, Chubby and Neil, who had had a distinguished one-day career with England, and a few of the players. They all said exactly the same thing – this was an opportunity I could not turn down.

I had captained England A and the Under 19s and although there was always going to be the issue of whether the captaincy would affect my batting, I felt the job would offer more benefits than debits – particularly as I hadn't exactly set the word alight in the one-day game. For me, the overriding consideration was the chance to make a mark on the English game. I imagined that being captain would allow me to have a major say in taking a new team forward. Although I quickly discovered how difficult it is to get decisions taken in a committee-run organisation, I feel that if I can have some positive effect in that direction, it will be an achievement. Apart from that, I like the fact that, as captain, the decisions you take on the pitch can influence the outcome of a match. I enjoy that kind of responsibility.

When the call finally came through, David Graveney said, 'We fancy you for the job. Will you accept it?' I said, 'Of course.' He called back the following morning and the job was mine. I had to go to Lord's and have my picture taken against a backdrop of photographs of all the previous one-day captains. That brought home just what an honour it was and I came out with the spiel that every captain delivers when he gets the job.

There were a host of congratulatory messages. I treasured them all but none more than the one from David English, whose Bunburys, an international celebrity team, do so much for youth cricket in this country. David extracted the proverbial in customary fashion.

I really had no idea what I was letting myself in for. The role of one-day captain is more important than it has ever been, and more in the spotlight. As a player, even if I'd played well, I could still enjoy some privacy, but as soon as I was appointed captain it seemed that everybody knew me and wanted to know more. As a player, you don't quite realise what the captain has to put up with.

For example, I don't think there have ever been as many cameras at grounds as there are today and one of them is always trained on the captain whether he's batting, in the field or in the dressing room. There is probably only one room free of cameras – I suppose even television directors realise some things are best done in private. The prying eyes are trying to spot any weaknesses in the captain's armour or any secrets he may give away. You know you are being watched constantly and that makes the job incredibly intense, but it cannot detract from the massive buzz that comes from leading your country out at Lord's.

Out on the field, we made a clear statement that we were trying to build towards the 2007 World Cup. The way to gain the confidence to do that is by winning games, and to triumph in our first series in June 2003 against Pakistan was wonderful for everybody, particularly as Pakistan are a very good one-day side. A tremendous effort was needed after losing the first game at Old Trafford. To come back and win at The Oval and then to go to Lord's and win the final was a tremendous achievement. Trescothick played two of the best one-day knocks you are ever likely to see anywhere. There was a real buzz about the team – a youthful feel of exuberance and excitement. I kept telling them to go out and enjoy their cricket. I know it's hard in front of big crowds and under pressure, but enjoyment was the key factor. My message to the players was not to put more pressure on themselves, but just to go out and enjoy giving it their best shot. I wanted the English dressing room to be somewhere the players entered with their heads up at all times.

When I first got the job, we were thinking more for the future than the present and when you do that you are bound to make mistakes. As a young team the important thing is to learn quickly from errors and I encouraged the players to prepare as thoroughly as possible, enjoy the occasion and let their instincts and natural talents take over without worrying unduly.

I am the captain and I make the decisions, but I shouldn't be the only one out there thinking about the game and tactics. Every player should be doing that. I now understand why Nasser sometimes got riled on the field and occasionally became a victim of his frustrations. I was one of those who probably didn't help him enough and left him on his own, especially when times were hard. For too long, I wasn't confident enough in my own ability, so I didn't say anything to Nasser. It was only in his last year in charge, when I played really well and felt I could offer a little bit of advice, that I talked more to him. I thought other players could have helped more, too. He was very good anyway, but when there's a big opposing partnership and you can see players with their heads down, not wanting to get involved, it must have got to him. We can't have that. Everybody has to be involved at all stages. It's easy to fly around making helpful suggestions when you're taking wickets – we can all do that. It's when the going gets tough that the players have to dig in. I have told them that we work together as a team, from youngest to oldest. If someone has an idea, don't come up after every ball, but whisper in my ear at the change over and if I think it's a good idea, I'll go with it. If I don't, I'll say why I don't like it.

Martyn Moxon was my first captain with Yorkshire. I was eighteen and in awe of the entire set-up – and him. He had his own leadership style, but I was so young I kept my head down, hardly said a word and tried to play my own game, so I didn't study how he went about things.

David 'Bingo' Byas was his successor. David was straight talking, open and honest and sometimes pretty aggressive, a tough man who liked to run a disciplined ship. He wanted smartness, good timekeeping and the team to work very hard on their fitness levels. I agree with all of that because if you are disciplined off the pitch you will be on it, but I also appreciate that not every player is exactly the same. There are those who will always be on time and smart and you know you won't have to worry about them, and there are those who are not like that. They will be late occasionally, scruffy and forget things. I actually don't mind that type at all. In fact, the more different types you have in a dressing room, the better the place is. If we were all stereotyped robots doing exactly the same it would be bloody boring.

Having beaten Pakistan, we were confident going into the summer one-day tournament against South Africa, who are a fantastic one-day side, and Zimbabwe, who are capable of beating anybody on their day.

The Springboks gave us a good hiding at Old Trafford after

we had hammered them at The Oval, thanks mainly to Trescothick, who played exceptionally well throughout the summer, as did Jimmy Anderson with the ball.

One real spark in the team was the way the lads fielded. I put a lot of emphasis on us being a young, energetic team in the field and it seemed to pay off. We got a number of run-outs and some great catches. There was great enthusiasm within the team and that must continue. A team has to be energised all the time, especially in the one-day arena, where you have to be full of tricks. I have always been a thinking player, even if I didn't give many ideas to Nasser, so in a way the one-day captaincy came as second nature to me. Now I feel I'm just steering the ship. I thoroughly enjoy working out field settings, which bowler to use against different batsmen, when to take fielders out and when to bring them back in.

We lost our first match with Zimbabwe in the three-nation event and our next one, at Headingley, was rained off, but we came back strongly to beat them at Bristol. We also lost one game against South Africa but beat them twice, and went on to defeat them again in the final, which was as good a one-day performance as has been seen for many a match. So at the end of the two one-day series that summer of 2003, we ended up with two trophies, which was fantastic because it brought a good feeling about the team and English cricket.

However, although we had played some wonderful cricket, I was realistic enough to understand that we were still miles away from being the best team in the world. We got a bit of praise, but I knew we still had a long way to go on our roller-coaster journey to the 2007 World Cup.

A few weeks later, the five Test series against South Africa meant a return to the ranks for me because Nasser was still in charge. After the one-day final against South Africa, Nasser had been the first person on the phone to say well done. He told me not to underestimate what I'd done over the three weeks of the tournament. It was nice of him to say that, especially as when he turned up at Edgbaston for the First Test, I think it was hard for him. We had a young team including a lot of guys I'd just captained with some success and they were still regarding me as being in charge. Nasser may have felt that he'd lost his team a little bit.

My form had suffered after becoming one-day captain, as I thought it might. Throughout the summer I didn't play well. I scored a hundred for Yorkshire but didn't feel in great touch. In the one-day games I was really fighting for form, especially against Zimbabwe, although I didn't do too badly in the end, and I was still struggling in the First Test. I may have ended up with 156 but when I look back, the first 20 runs were probably as hard a 20 as I've ever scored. I had a huge confrontation with Shaun Pollock on the third morning when I batted for about eighty minutes without scoring, but I dug in, got a big score and the match was drawn.

When we arrived on the Monday, there was a lot of talking in the coaches' room and I could see Nasser's head was down. I was devouring a bacon buttie when Duncan Fletcher called me in and told me Nasser was thinking about resigning and asked if I was up for the job if it became available. I said I was, but David Graveney said they didn't think it was the right time for Nasser to go and would try to persuade him to stay on. It wasn't clear whether they wanted him for the rest of the summer or just the next Test, which was due to start at Lord's that Thursday, 31 July. However, Nasser would not be turned and the vacant post was quickly offered to me. The Lord's Test was always going to be a difficult match, given that we had one day to prepare, but now the country had a new captain as well.

South Africa's captain Graeme Smith, new to the role himself, won the toss and sent us in on a wicket that looked typical of Lord's. The side batting first often make 350 to 400, but we contrived to get bowled out for 173 and were chasing the game from the moment our last wicket fell all too prematurely.

Nasser dropped Smith on 8 and he went on to get 259. Everything that could go wrong did so and we were frustratingly consistent – we batted badly, bowled badly and fielded badly while they showed better application and more determination although Freddie Flintoff smashing a hundred on the Sunday did give us a bit of a lift.

Most of the time we were out in the field, being hit everywhere, and I couldn't see a wicket coming. The thought did run through my head, 'What on earth have I taken on here?' I knew that Gough was thinking about retiring and there were whispers that Nasser was going as well. I wondered what was going on – we were getting hammered in a Test, struggling like hell, and two top players were possibly going to retire.

It was important that I had a chat with Nasser just to set the record straight and discover what his plans were. He said it had been a hard week, emotionally as much as anything, and that all he could say at that moment was that he was going to back me to the hilt and wanted to continue playing, which was great news. In the next game at Trent Bridge he got a hundred, which typifies the kind of character he is.

That next match was a huge game for us. We won the toss and Mark Butcher and Nasser played very well. We had South Africa under pressure before allowing them to get somewhere close to us. The wicket was deteriorating when they started the final innings needing 202. The Monday was going to be one of the biggest days of my career because we just had to win. If we'd gone 2–0 down, we'd have been absolutely screwed. They needed 152 with six wickets left – but cometh the hour, cometh James Kirtley. The Sussex paceman bowled extremely well, putting the ball in the right areas to take us to victory.

Going to Headingley with the series level at 1–1, I thought we had a massive opportunity to draw ahead. We'd brought in Surrey's Martin Bicknell for his experience. At the home of Yorkshire cricket, consistently putting the ball on the spot is what takes wickets. Pace is not generally a huge factor.

When we had them at 142 for 7, it looked as though we'd bowl them out cheaply and then have the use of the wicket at its best, on the second day and half of the third. Credit must go to South Africa's Gary Kirsten for a fantastic hundred – and Zondeki got 50 odd – but we missed a great chance. We let the game drift away from us. They got too many runs, we didn't bat well and there was controversy when Butcher and Trescothick opted to come off for bad light when they were going well. The forecast for the next day was good so why risk losing a couple of wickets that night? With two of our most experienced players at the crease, I didn't feel the need to be sending out signals. They knew how well they could see the ball, but we were on top and it gave South Africa the chance to regroup. They came out the following day, got a couple of quick wickets and finally bashed us.

In the one-day matches we'd been up one minute and down the next and here it was the same at full Test level. I don't think anybody expected us to come back at The Oval. I remember the jeers from the crowd on the first day when they were smashing us everywhere. Gibbs hit a fantastic century, but two late wickets gave us a glimmer. They were 350 for 4 at the end of the day's play and our odds had gone to 40–1. They went on to 484 and you don't see many teams winning a Test match facing that kind of total.

We knew we had to bat for a long time and Trescothick scored a magnificent double century. Graham Thorpe was back in the team because Nasser was injured and it was fantastic to see him get a ton, but Trescothick's double was the backbone of the innings. It allowed Flintoff to go out and score an unbelievable 95, which swayed the balance in our favour that Sunday morning. The way Freddie took the game away from the Springboks was fantastic and we ended up with a lead of just over 100. I knew that if we had a lead, no matter how many, we could put them under pressure.

Steve Harmison bowled a great spell to get rid of Kallis and Kirsten but we still needed a handful of wickets. Martin Bicknell obliged as we knocked them over and set about chasing a target of 109 to win. It was the best Test match I'd ever played in – great weather, great crowd, great game. It was also Alec Stewart's last international match. I said to the lads before we went out for the final day that Alec had started his Test career with a win and we wanted to send the great man away with one. 'If anybody deserves a victorious send-off, it's him,' I said.

I felt I was getting better as a captain although I hadn't scored as many runs since I'd got the job, but whether you are captain or not you go through dips in form. My energies were probably not focused as they should have been. Meetings, phone calls, all the things that go with the captaincy that you don't appreciate as a player are very draining but, to be honest, when I got the Test job I probably got involved in all kinds of issues I'd have been better out of. I was scoring 20 to 25 and playing iffy shots, which I hadn't done for quite a while. I was tired and not in rhythm, and my footwork was not as good as I like it to be. But 2–2 against a very good South Africa team, with one drawn match, was not a bad start. We were quite inexperienced in the bowling department and to get them out twice on a flat Oval wicket was a great way to finish the summer.

Our next stop was the sub-continent and I realised that my number one role in Bangladesh and Sri Lanka during the winter of 2003 was to start scoring runs again. Thankfully, I was top scorer in the Bangladesh series and bagged most runs in Sri Lanka. My first hundred as captain came at Kandy. It was a very special moment against a tough team in their own backyard. Throughout those two series – and the coaches will bear this out – my balance and play were better than they had been in Australia the previous winter, which was a good sign.

Overall, the most important thing is to get the England team to play together regularly. For the last few years, we have had to make a lot of changes because of injuries, but South Africa's team, Australia's, Sri Lanka's and India's never seem to vary much and the sooner we can get a settled side the better. That may entail a change in the structure of the game – my predecessors Bob Willis, Michael Atherton, Alec Stewart and Nasser have all said as much. Maybe by the time my successor steps in, or even while I'm still captain, we will be producing a lot more players like the Aussies, who come straight into a county or Test team and score a hundred on debut. At the moment we don't know what our best team is because we have so many young players. The batsmen generally pick themselves, but we must quickly develop our bowling attack. We need something just a little bit different.

My baptism as England captain was one of fire. Now I am more aware than ever of what comes with the job. If the team wins, the captain is brilliant, even though he might have done nothing with bat or ball. When the team loses, the captain's lousy even though he may have done all he possibly could to avoid defeat. In other words, when you lose you take a lot of stick that is often unfounded, and when you win you get praise that you probably don't deserve. But come what may, I've come to appreciate that the captain cannot be a miracle worker and should concentrate on his number one job, which is to get eleven players out on the pitch and direct what goes on there. Everything else should be looked after by other people.

Whatever happens, the memory of my year in the sun and its aftermath will never fade. I may never have another time like it. All I know is that I will do everything I can to build on those achievements in a bid to ensure England's future is brighter than it has been for a long time.

Test Record from Ahmedabad 2001 to Sydney 2003

Runs	How Out	Test	Opponents & Venue	Date
11	caught	2nd	India at Ahmedabad	11/12/2001
64	handled	3rd	India at Bangalore	19/12/2001
27	caught wk	1st	New Zealand at Christchurch	13/03/2002
7	caught	2nd	New Zealand at Wellington	21/03/2002
34	caught			
27	caught wk	3rd	New Zealand at Auckland	30/03/2002
36	caught			
64	caught	1st	Sri Lanka at Lord's	16/05/2002
115	caught wk			
46	caught	2nd	Sri Lanka at Birmingham	30/05/2002
36	caught	3rd	Sri Lanka at Manchester	13/06/2002
24*	not out			
0	lbw	1st	India at Lord's	25/07/2002
100	caught			
197	caught wk	2nd	India at Nottingham	08/08/2002
61	caught	3rd	India at Leeds	22/08/2002
15	lbw			
195	caught wk	4th	India at The Oval	05/09/2002
47*	not out			
33	caught wk	1st	Australia at Brisbane	07/11/2002
0	lbw			
177	caught	2nd	Australia at Adelaide	21/11/2002
41	caught			
34	caught wk	3rd	Australia at Perth	29/11/2002
9	run out			
11	bowled	4th	Australia at Melbourne	26/12/2002
145	caught			
0	caught wk	5th	Australia at Sydney	02/01/2003
183	lbw			

One-Day International Record from Calcutta 2002 to the ICC World Cup 2003

Runs	How Out	ODI	Opponents & Venue	Date
14	caught	1st	India at Calcutta	19/01/2002
63	run out	2nd	India at Cuttack	22/01/2002
43	caught	3rd	India at Chennai	25/01/2002
4	bowled	4th	India at Kanpur	28/01/2002
7*	not out	5th	India at Delhi	31/01/2002
16	stumped	6th	India at Mumbai	03/02/2002
59	run out	4th	New Zealand at Auckland	23/02/2002
DNB	–	NW Series 5	India at Chester-le-Street	04/07/2002
14	caught	NW Series 7	Sri Lanka at Manchester	07/07/2002
30	caught	NW Series 8	India at The Oval	09/07/2002
3	caught	NW Series F	India at Lord's	13/07/2002
28	caught	VB Series 10	Sri Lanka at Adelaide	17/01/2003
21	caught wk	VB Series 11	Australia at Adelaide	19/01/2003
21	lbw	VB Series F1	Australia at Sydney	23/01/2003
60	caught	VB Series F2	Australia at Melbourne	25/01/2003
51	caught	World Cup 13	Netherlands at East London	16/02/2003
14	caught	World Cup 19	Namibia at Port Elizabeth	19/02/2003
52	caught	World Cup 23	Pakistan at Cape Town	22/02/2003
20	caught wk	World Cup 30	India at Durban	26/02/2003
2	caught wk	World Cup 37	Australia at Port Elizabeth	02/03/2003